❈ EXPERIENCE INTO THOUGHT ❈

THE ALEXANDER LECTURES

The Alexander Lectureship was founded in honour of Professor W.J. Alexander, who held the Chair of English at University College, University of Toronto, from 1889 to 1926. The Lectureship brings to the university a distinguished scholar or critic to give a course of lectures on a subject related to English literature.

KATHLEEN COBURN

Experience into Thought

PERSPECTIVES IN THE
COLERIDGE NOTEBOOKS

UNIVERSITY OF TORONTO PRESS
Toronto   Buffalo   London

Library of Congress Cataloging in Publication Data

Coburn, Kathleen.
Experience into thought.

(The Alexander lectures)
Includes bibliographical references and index.
1. Coleridge, Samuel Taylor, 1772 – 1834. Notebooks.
2. Coleridge, Samuel Taylor, 1772 – 1834 – Criticism and
interpretation.   I. Title. II. Series: Toronto. University.
Alexander Foundation. The Alexander lectures.
PR4483.A393C58   821'.7   78-32099
ISBN 0-8020-5449-8

This book has been published with the help of grants from the
Canadian Federation for the Humanities, using funds provided by the
Social Sciences and Humanities Research Council of Canada, and
the Publications Fund of University of Toronto Press.

To the memory of
PELHAM EDGAR
and
GEORGE SIDNEY BRETT
two teachers with creative imagination

❄❂❄ CONTENTS ❄❂❄

Mr. Coleridge talks of himself without being an egotist, for in him the individual is always merged in the abstract and general.

Hazlitt

When I got there, the organ was playing the 100th psalm and, when it was done, Mr. Coleridge rose and gave out his text, 'And he went up into the mountain to pray, HIMSELF, ALONE.' As he gave out his text, his voice 'rose like a steam of rich distilled perfumes,' and when he came to the two last words, which he pronounced loud, deep, and distinct, it seemed to me, who was then young, as if the sounds had echoed from the bottom of the human heart, and as if that prayer might have floated in solemn silence through the universe.

Hazlitt

❧❦ ABBREVIATIONS ❧❦

❧ LECTURE ONE ❧

✵ LECTURE ONE ✵

'**I**T IS A COMMON DELUSION that Coleridge is well-known.' That was said in the 1850s in Cambridge, Coleridge's own university, by F.J.A. Hort. Though Coleridge was always much cited, quoted, and either honoured or reviled, Hort's dictum about him and his public is still today almost as true as it was then, but not quite.[1] The very invitation to lecture on him in this distinguished series is evidence of a change since the 1930s when both in this university and in Oxford the authorities tried to dissuade me from studying Coleridge as a thinker, and to turn my post-graduate work towards Wordsworth; there were no supervisors ready to consider Coleridge a serious subject in himself. Nor were they peculiar in this. The situation was the same almost everywhere. Yet G.S. Brett and Pelham Edgar had aroused my curiosity about Coleridge first as a philosopher and critic. I gratefully take this opportunity on home ground to record my debt to them.

When I asked my friend Barker Fairley what I should speak about in these lectures, he said, 'Tell what interests you in Coleridge.' Others less politely have sometimes asked, 'How on earth have you stood him all these years?'

In fact, I have been increasingly interested to find Coleridge a person and thinker very different from the historical and public impression of him – more lonely, more rebellious, more sceptical, much wider in range, and more deeply human.

Coleridge was born in 1772, and all his life rebelled in a

---

1 In October 1975, I noticed one of the candidates in a BBC quiz chose as his special subject, 'The Life and Works of S.T. Coleridge.' And in the Edinburgh Festival Fringe in July 1977, of 400 shows Coleridge was the inspiration for two – a new play by Leonard Maguire and a dance-mime interpretation of the *Ancient Mariner*.

multitude of ways, but especially against the narrow rationalism of the eighteenth century, 'this enlightened century' as he scoffingly called it, into which he was born. Like most rebels he also partook of the mother's milk he rejected, and was never free of the inevitable conflicts and inconsistencies. There are therefore many Coleridges. If I may assume (as Coleridge in my place would have done) that my books are largely unread, perhaps I may risk repetition in giving a little list of the various dynamos that go by the name 'Coleridge.'

First the poet (but known chiefly for only three miraculous poems and about three others); then the literary critic, without whom the history of English literary criticism as we know it is inconceivable; the critic of science, the 'so-so chemist' as he called himself, whose rôle in sharing the struggle of Davy and others over the concepts and terminology of modern chemistry and biology is just beginning to be appreciated; the logician, whose hitherto unpublished *Logic*, edited by Professor Robin Jackson, is in the hands of the printers;[2] the journalist, the top leader-writer of his day in the *Morning Post* and the *Courier*, whose three volumes of newspaper contributions will reappear any day now;[3] the social and political critic, who wrote the first analysis in English of a post-war economic depression at the close of the Napoleonic wars, a work admired by Maynard Keynes; the psychologist, who grasped the notion of a subconscious mental life and of varying levels of consciousness, who coined the words *psycho-analytical*[4] and *psycho-somatic*[5] (as well as hundreds of other words now in our dictionaries), who anticipated the twentieth century on dreams; the educationist, who believed in cultivating the

2 To be published Autumn 1979
3 Published in 1978
4 *CN* II 2670
5 *IS* § 52

initiative in children and attacked the conventional negative controls by punishment; in theology the 'higher critic,' who ploughed methodically through dozens of the heavy German volumes of Eichhorn, Michaelis, and their ilk, and advocated an historical approach to Judaism and Christianity, denouncing what he called the 'superstitious' reading of the Scriptures; and one of the most influential of all Coleridges, the analyst of the church as both a spiritual and a temporal society, and of the obligations of both church and state to the national culture; and there is Coleridge the Englishman who was a determined 'cosmopolite' (to use another word he coined), who drew up a plan for a league of nations (admittedly with a proviso – although the Napoleonic wars were over – that no Frenchman be allowed to settle outside France or her colonies). And I see I had almost forgotten the philosopher! Yet he delivered possibly the first course of public lectures by an Englishman on the history of that subject – for money (not much money).

Why, I am often asked, have we not been more adequately aware of these many Coleridges?

One reason is that Coleridge was long ago appropriated by the literary and – frequently the fate of poets – was therefore considered something of a freak in other fields. Even now the monographs issuing from English departments on him as poet and literary critic far exceed in number all the rest, creating the impression that there lies his chief importance. Some of the most learned Coleridgians – Owen Barfield and Thomas McFarland for instance – do not think so. Wilfred Hindle said, in his history of the *Morning Post*, that the best memorial that could be raised to Coleridge would be the republication of his contributions to that paper; in a survey of English religious opinion in the nineteenth century Bernard Reardon said of his pre-eminence as a religious thinker, 'virtually all of his immediate British contemporaries seem to belong to a

5

different [and by implication, inferior] intellectual world.'[6] As long ago as 1929 Joseph Needham in a volume of essays entitled *The Sceptical Biologist* was moved to write one of the ten essays on 'Coleridge as a Philosophic Biologist' and while he gives a grade of about a B plus to Coleridge he credits him as biologist with some profundity in his attacks on contemporary science and its logic, and with having anticipated in a general way the idea of emergent evolution. William Walsh sees Coleridge's chief contribution to his own and more recent times as lying in his writings on education and the application of his general views in that field. There are many such specialist treatments of Coleridge – but very few attempts to see the broader picture.[7] We are all impressed with *Coleridge's Variety*,[8] but who has coped with that variety? The fault may lie in ourselves, but it lies at least partly in Coleridge's stars.

When he died in 1834 at the age of sixty-two he left to his executors, the surgeon Joseph Henry Green, his son-in-law and nephew Henry Nelson Coleridge, and his son Derwent, a vast chaos of manuscripts; many more had been scattered casually to the winds in the chancy possession of friends and relations. There were some seventy notebooks, about eight hundred annotated books (some heavily so) and shoals of sibylline leaves detached from any mooring whatsoever, together with certain volumes of manuscripts known to be parts of projected works (either in Coleridge's holograph or dictated by him to various amanuenses). Mr Green was to prepare for publication the philosophical remains, the Reverend Derwent the theological, and Henry Nelson Coleridge

6 *From Coleridge to Gore* (1971) 72
7 Yet see Gordon Mackenzie *Organic Unity in Coleridge* (1939); Richard Haven *Patterns of Consciousness* (1969); Owen Barfield *What Coleridge Thought* (1971).
8 The title of a collection of bicentenary lectures in Cambridge in 1972 edited by John Beer

the literary materials – and so right there the dividing up of Coleridge into departments began.

In the first three years of their labours two events took place which influenced their decisions. The first now seems unimportant enough, but not to them. In 1837 Joseph Cottle published his *Early Recollections Chiefly Relating to the Late S. T. Coleridge.* This benefactor of the young Coleridge and Wordsworth and Southey, whose real claim to fame is that he published the *Lyrical Ballads*, was a generous but vain and ill-educated man. He glowed in the stimulating company of the young poets, but perhaps later took some kind of vengeance for their (hardly concealed) jokes at his expense. (E.g. Coleridge: 'strange there are no female philosophers.' Cottle: 'what about Moll Branche?') Possibly Cottle, having picked some winners, was just using his memoirs to gather in the returns on his bets. However it was, he spilled garrulously in print the tale of what he called, with typical inaccuracy, Coleridge's 'unhappy passion for Opium.' Then, a decade later, as a result of the ensuing feud, he poured salt on the scratches, publishing in 1847 his *Reminiscences of Coleridge and Southey.* That Cottle also said Coleridge's 'frantic passion for opium was eventually overcome' did not mitigate his crassness in the eyes of the first family editors. He made them not only cautious but defensive and selective.

The second event, Victoria's ascent to the throne in 1837, meant that their task coincided with the onset of the Victorian virtues. STC, or Uncle Sam, as they called him, the best-known and most conspicuously brilliant member of the family, had to be presented to the public in as respectable a light as possible. Many highly regarded citizens took opium – Wilberforce, for instance. Coleridge's addiction had for decades been no secret to his wide circle of friends, but Cottle's revelation somehow besmirched him in print. And as Cottle the benefactor made clear, Coleridge and Southey wore the additional disgrace of having been penniless radicals in youth, even though Southey was now the poet laureate and Coleridge in the later years of his life had been sought out by the most respectable visitors from all over the world. No wonder the editing of the manuscript materials, to which the family had full access, presented problems of selection which they solved according to their Victorian tastes. Coleridge had always been a blot on the family escutcheon. They would now whiten his reputation to match the silvery locks of the Oracle of Highgate.

So the first work produced after Coleridge's death – apart from the 1834 *Poems* even then in the press – was the *Table Talk* (1835). HNC had the wit to make himself his uncle's Boswell, but Coleridge's elder son, Hartley, protested on publication that his father had been more liberal, not so High Church and Tory as the *Table Talk* made him. Crabb Robinson also complained against it that STC had always distinguished between *goodiness* and *goodness*, and that HNC had made him 'a goody man.' It is not necessary for me to recite the whole story of the early editing, but suffice it to say that the editors' selections were made according to their tastes and times, and in general were unconsciously distorted in the direction of maintaining the family views. Sara Coleridge ('the most beautiful and the most learned woman of her day' it was said) shared with her father a taste and a reputation for obscure erudition and she would have found it natural to stress that reputation. No doubt they did not always grasp the scope of some of Coleridge's more far-sighted and comprehensive observations – not even Sara, the best of the first-generation editors – nor did they follow the sharp points of his insights especially in psychological matters. Much of the best, most lively, and most original material was left unpublished. Even when some of it was printed, in the four volumes of *Literary Remains* for instance (under that morgue-like title), somehow, by little touchings-up, the fragments, marginalia, and lecture notes lost in the process some of the crackle and flash of their lightning. From one cause or another the impression of Coleridge was the old Peacockian view that saw him living in Mr Flosky's clouds rather than in the real world.[9] In the twentieth century, on the other hand, Lowes, Cecil Bald, Herbert Read, Humphry House, John Bayley, I.A. Richards, L.C. Knights – to refer to the elders only – all stress Coleridge's gift for precision and see his method as rooted in the specific perceived world.

One must be chary however in criticizing by hindsight these early attempts at putting a giant with seven-league boots within the confines of print and book covers. (For one thing, one's own turn will come!) The early editors had a formidable, irrepressible polymath to put in order; their assiduity and devotion were as energetic as their circumstances (and healths) allowed. But John Stuart Mill said rightly, in 1840, the mood of the time was not ready for Coleridge.

Mill wrote one of the better early essays on Coleridge, but he was greatly influenced by HNC's review of the 1834 *Poems* in the *Quarterly Review* (to all intents and purposes his own edition when Coleridge was at death's door) and so even Mill was taken in by HNC's Tory emphasis. It is in fact a mark of Mill's brilliance (and Coleridge's power) that Coleridge the inquirer stands so high in Mill's estimate. We must regard the prejudices of the family editors as a warning to ourselves, but also as an explanation of why, more than a hundred years on, there is a particular need of a new Coleridge. The Coleridge of the notebooks, the marginalia, many manuscript fragments, the unpublished 'opus maximum' and many other unknowns,

9 There was a short period of fresh interest, near the turn of the century, around the publication of the *Letters* and *Anima Poetae* by Coleridge's grandson. Walter Pater, e.g., was aware of Coleridge's unusual sensibility.

is a stronger Coleridge. Even some prose works long in print, and some of the poems, will take on a different light when seen in the new perspective. The *Collected Works* sponsored by Bollingen Foundation will run to more than twenty-five volumes, not counting the five volumes of *Notebooks*. But then Coleridge himself said that each generation must rediscover the poets anew.

To justify the adjective 'stronger' I once thought to reply at this point to the two common attacks on Coleridge, revived quite recently – opium addiction and plagiarisms from the Germans. But I remembered a notebook entry that fits the case, in which Coleridge quotes Blumenbach as saying of the attacks of a medical adversary, 'Multum hic veri, multum novi; sed quod est verum, non novum est, quod est novum non verum est.' (Much here is true, much new, but what is true is not new and what is new is not true.) No. Anyone who has lived his way through the marginalia and the notebooks, especially, but the published works as well, will be the last to cry 'cheat.'

Far more interesting than the pursuit of all the charges and accusations, whether Coleridge is vulnerable to them or not, is to look at what he did with the facts of his experiences as he encountered them, in books or on his flesh. It is not Coleridge the critic, the poet, the philosopher, the public servant, the newspaper man, the psychologist I wish chiefly to present in these lectures; all these men, all called Coleridge, will appear indirectly, but I would have you see his rare capacity to experience, to recognize, and to participate in the experiences life brought to him and he brought to life. In the notebooks and marginalia he commanded a remarkable ability to articulate them. There is a special quality in his curiosity, a certain toughness of mind, a scepticism if you will, and over it all his original ways of relating one thought to another.

In the remainder of this lecture I should like to read some

notebook entries that show the early development of a sense of isolation, contributing to that awareness of experience in which certain creative trends of consciousness developed, certain activities of mind, and in particular an acute sense of the gap between appearances – on all fronts – and reality.

In an outsize 'notebook' called the 'Folio Notebook' (Coleridge is full of contradictions) there is an autobiographical fragment written two years before his death for his friend and medical adviser James Gillman. Coleridge was sixty years old at the time. The entry begins with characteristic particularity.

Friday Night, 9 March 1832 Mem. Capital bronzed Pen from Mr Bage's.

Coleridge had generally used quill pens, often filched for him by Charles Lamb from the India House. There follows a desperate attempt at order:

Retrospect, fragments of, 1. Early Childhood. The last child, the youngest Child of Ten by the same Mother [and he names them all]... and the 13th taking in the three Sisters by my dear Father's first Wife...

The youngest Child, possibly inheriting the commencing decay of musculo-arterial Power in my Father who died in his 62nd year when I had not yet reached my 7th...

I skip some quaint physiological terms and speculations that show he felt he was the runt of the litter. He then goes on:

And certainly, from the Jealousy of old Molly [the nurse] and by the infusions of her Jealousy into my Brother's [Francis's, the next older sibling's] mind, I was in earliest childhood lifted away from the enjoyments of muscular activity – from Play – to take refuge at my

11

mother's side on my little stool, to read my little books and to listen to the Talk of my Elders – I was driven from Life in Motion to Life in Thought and sensation. I never played except by myself, and then only acting over what I had been reading or fancying, or half one, half the other, with a stick cutting down the Weeds & Nettles, as one of the Seven Champions of Christendom. Alas! I had all the simplicity, all the docility of a little Child; but none of the Child's Habits – I never thought as a Child; never had the language of a Child. –

Note the solitariness, the paranoia, the acting out of the fantasy of the strong man, champion of the oppressed.

I forget whether it was in my 5th or 6th year, but I believe the latter, in consequence of some quarrel between me and my Brother, it was in the first week of October, I ran away – from fear of being whipt and passed the whole night, a night of rain and storm, on the bleak side of a Hill on the River Otter, & was found, alive but without the power of my limbs, at day-break about six yards from the naked banks of the River – The consequence, a remittent, and then a rheumatic fever –

Note that half a century later, the child's long dark night of runaway miseries is still vivid.

He then tells of his father's death of which he had premonitions that frightened him and made him feel half-guilty of it. He was then placed in Christ's Hospital junior school. The blue uniform was (and still is) an orphanage costume dating back to the foundation in 1552.

... O what a change! – Deprest, moping, friendless poor Orphan, half-starved (at that time the portion of food given to the Blue-coats was cruelly insufficient for those who had no friends to supply them – from 8 to 14 I was a playless Day-dreamer, an Helluo Librorum, my appetite for which was indulged by a singular Inci-

dent, a stranger who struck by my conversation made me free of a [...]
great Circulating Library in King's Street, Cheapside – I *read thro* the
whole Catalogue, folios and all – whether I understood them or did
not understand them – running all risks, in skulking out, to get the
two Volumes which I was entitled to have daily – Conceive what I
must have been at 14 – I had never played – I was in a continued low
fever – my whole Being was with eyes closed to every object of *present*
sense – to crumple myself up in a sunny Corner, and read, read, read,
– finding myself in Rob. Crusoe's Island, finding a Mountain of Plum
Cake, and eating out a room for myself, and then eating it into the
shapes of Chairs & Tables – Hunger and Fancy –

The playless daydreamer again, undernourished with food –
substituting the oral activity of excessive reading –
becoming a Robinson Crusoe of the mind, 'eyes closed to
every object of sense.' But note the daydream of *making*; the
plum-cake room had tables and chairs, in the plural, for
sociability.

He confesses to classroom precociousness over and above
the other boys, and bemoans

the measureless difference between me and them in the wide, wild
wilderness of useless, unarranged Book-knowlege, and book-
thoughts... at 14 or at 12 I should have made as pretty a juvenile
Prodigy as was ever emasculated & ruined by fond and idle wonder-
ment. Thank Heaven! I was flogged, instead of flattered.

Notice his awareness of the lack of motivation, to which he
often referred later as his diseased Will; also the reservations
about knowledge that is 'Book-knowlege,' and thoughts that
are 'Book-Thoughts.'

The first welcome excitements of motivation (but he recog-
nizes it as fleeting) came when on Saturdays he was allowed to
walk the London Hospital with his brother Luke – and was

allowed to assist at a bedside! Suddenly he had an aim, began to read everything medical – English, Latin, and Greek – and when that proved 'a wild dream' his reading turned to metaphysics, sceptical metaphysics – and theology – Cato's Letters, Voltaire.

In my 16th year I had made friends – a Widow Lady, who had a Son, whom I as upper Boy had protected, took to me & taught me what it was to have a Mother. I loved her as such – she had three daughters – & I, of course, fell in love – & with the eldest – & from this time to my 19th when I quitted School for Jesus, Cambridge, was the *aera* of poetry & love.

Note that he fell in love with the family warmth he had missed. Possibly much too much has been read into the failure of the Mary Evans affair. One must perhaps add that if the love was as commonplace as the poetry he wrote at the time (1788-91) one can estimate the affair as pallid. However, he does describe this period of puberty as bringing a great change for the better:

But from the exuberance of my animal Spirits, when I had burst forth from my misery & mopery, and the indiscretions resulting from these spirits, – ex gr. swimming in the New River in my Clothes & remaining in them full half the time – from 17 to 18 was passed in the Sick Ward, Jaundice, and Rheumatic Fever –

Youth & commencing Manhood –

Went to Jesus [College Cambridge] – for the first term, & as long as Middleton was at Pembroke (later Bishop of Calcutta) read hard, got the Greek Ode

He means he won a prize for a Greek ode on the slave trade. Note the capacity for work if a friend was near by; the chief point of literary interest in the Greek ode is Coleridge's personal identification with the slaves.

Then there was the stupid episode of letting some tradesman furnish his rooms – in total ignorance of the correct procedures – and getting into what felt like very deep debt. The guilt was – as usual with Coleridge – absurdly out of proportion to the deed, and as he says he

became miserable – drank bad wine – & volunteered the credit of vices of which I was *not* guilty – A dreary time of self-reproach, and bewilderment followed ... in the agitation of mind & its consequences my Constitution assuredly was arrested in its efforts to establish itself.

He passes over the episode of the flight from Cambridge to the Light Dragoons, and so may we – except to add that one of the most prolonged hauntings that came out of it was that he was extricated from the military by his family on grounds of insanity. It was a face-saving device for officialdom and the family preferred to think of him as 'mad' rather than 'bad.' But that fear of insanity never left him.

There are but few lines more of this autobiography, the chief further comments being on his 'domestic sorrow & unquiet,' a fine euphemism for his cruelly unlucky marriage, and then on his ill health and the opium-taking.

Subject to bowel complaints – among the least, uneasiness of mind was not felt in the mind but in the lesser bowels, or above the region of the heart – At last, my knees began to swell – & for some months after my return from Germany & my establishment at Greta Hall, Keswick, I had been all but bed-ridden; when my old taste returning, for the study of medical works, having borrowed a load of old Medical Journals from my Medical Attendant, Mr Edmonson, I found – i.e. I fancied I found a case precisely like my own – in which a marvellous cure had been effected by rubbing in laudanum, at the same time that a dose was administered inwardly – / I tried it – It answered like a charm / in a day I was alive – all alive! – Wretched Delusion! – but I owe it in justice to myself to declare before God, that this – the curse and slavery of my life, did not commence in any low craving for sensation, in any desire or wish to stimulate or exhilarate myself – in fact, my nervous spirits and my mental activity was such as never required it – but wholly in rashness, and delusion, and presumptuous Quackery, and afterwards in pure *terror* – not *lured*, but goaded! – Bad enough as it is – God forgive me – the Penance has been most bitter –. [Folio Notebook]

Gillman knew all the rest, too well. Nor is it my intention to inflict on you much more of that biographical-psychological approach of which Owen Barfield complains, rightly, that it can become a substitute for trying to understand what Coleridge knew and thought. However, one can perhaps advantageously in the notebooks grasp in context what was and was *not* knowledge to Coleridge, what was book-knowledge and what were book-thoughts, real knowledge and real thoughts. In other words we do also need to look closely at his own analysis of his 'mode of becoming' if, as he said in the last chapter of *Biographia Literaria*, we know only 'by the act of becoming.'

Coleridge's 'mode of becoming' has far too often been traced solely to his reading. If the *Notebooks* as printed have distorted further the impression of Coleridge as 'an *Helluo Librorum*' – his own nicknames for himself had a way of sticking and they were almost all pejorative – perhaps these lectures give me the opportunity to put the emphasis right. For it is my main concern here to show that Coleridge *experienced* what he thought and *thought* only what he experienced. When he met his own thought or a similar experience in a book, as in a friend, he jumped for joy. In reading as in experiencing his was the great art of recognition, a surprisingly rare gift that goes with acute logicality.

The autobiographical entry makes evident Coleridge's own awareness of a split in his childhood experiences – at least one split. On the one hand there was the sense of the outer human world, largely painful, and very lonely – to the point of depriving him of many of the sheer physical sunshine joys of childhood. On the other there were the traumas of inner states, both painful and pleasant, from fantasies and day-dreams.

His own accounts make it clear that Coleridge's mental life in childhood was precocious, far in advance of his sensory experiences. When those did (rarely) come, they were rapturous:

... I remember, that at eight years old I walked with him (my father) one winter evening from a farmer's house, a mile from Ottery – & he told me the names of the stars – and how Jupiter was a thousand times larger than our world – and that the other twinkling stars were Suns that had worlds rolling round them – & when I came home, he shewed me how they rolled round – / . I heard him with a profound delight & admiration; but without the least mixture of wonder or incredulity. For from my early reading of Faery Tales, & Genii &c &c – my mind had been habituated *to the Vast* – & I never regarded *my senses* in any way as the criteria of my belief ... [*CL* I 354-5]

But then there came in his sixteenth year the effect of making friends for the first time – 'a bursting forth from misery & mopery' into the physical world the sensations of which were all the more exuberant for having been so long dammed up, so acute that to a conscience pre-disposed to guilt they were almost unbearable. By the time he was twenty-two he was writing to a friend: 'I would to God, that I too possessed

the tender irritableness of unhandled [?unbridled] Sensibility
– mine is a sensibility gangrened with inward corruption –'
and 'the keen searching of the air from without!'[10]

That the stresses of inner conflict did not destroy him was
owing in the main, I believe, to two characteristics that help
to make him interesting now, as they did to his friends in his
own time. His rebellion against the intellectual complacency
and social corruption of his day, hardened as the social 'cake
of custom' was in the seemingly endless reign of George III, his
distrust of the disparity between outer appearance and living
reality, made him an original and independent critic of that
society on every front. It is a mistake to think of Coleridge as a
rebel only in his youth; he was in some respects radical all his
life. The radicalism of his Cambridge days, wildly idealistic
and unrealistic though it may have been, probably helped to
stabilize his sanity. It gave an over-introspective lad those
saving outward thrusts of mind, from sympathy towards the
unconforming, the martyrs, the unrespected outcasts of var-
ious hues and times.

The other, less conspicuous but very potent characteristic
(it had its dark underside) was a gift for minute and searching
observation, an intellectual but not merely cerebral exercise
that gave the mental and emotional thrusts inward a quality
such as the world has seldom seen, even among poets. It is
impossible to exaggerate Coleridge's uncertainties about
himself and equally impossible to understand how, by what
mental and physical powers he was able, in the swirling
waters of self-doubt of which he was the vortex, to maintain
the degree and range of curiosity, psychological insight, and a
peculiarly objective introspection necessary to him as poet,

10 *CL* I 62, where the punctuation appears to be misleading: I have
substituted a dash for a comma.

critic, and philosopher. We look at it not as at an interesting case study, but because out of this self-scepticism and critical observation Coleridge built a poetry and a philosophy; and from it he reached out to other minds in which he saw similar struggles behind quite different achievements.

It is difficult in our post-Freud times to conceive what it was like two hundred years ago to think about mental anxieties and illnesses. Dr Battie's *Treatise on Madness* (1738) and his treatment of the mentally ill in asylums and 'mad houses' were still so little understood for decades as to give his name, Battie, in cruel popular usage, to his patients. What did it mean then to inquire 'how much lies *below* [man's] own Consciousness' (*CN* I 1554), a concept not easily grasped at any time? Yet in 1794 Coleridge referred to 'depths of Being, below, & radicative of, all Consciousness' (*CN* I 6). Such inquiries came out of his own experiences, including the horrors of the night. In the following notebook entry Coleridge is writing about marital unhappiness, and the frightening combined effect in sleep of 'Despair' and 'Hope,' and 'Guilt.' Something a bit like Macbeth's vision of Banquo's ghost, or Hamlet's of his father, seems to be present.

... Hence even in dreams of Sleep the Soul never *is*, because it either cannot or dare not be, any <ONE> THING; but lives in *approaches* – touched by the outgoing pre-existent Ghosts of many feelings – It feels for ever as a blind man with his protended Staff dimly thro' the medium of the instrument by which it pushes off, & in the act of repulsion, O for the eloquence of Shakspeare, who alone could feel & yet know how to embody these conceptions, with as curious a felicity as the thoughts are subtle. As if the finger which I saw with eyes had, as it were, another finger invisible – Touching me with a ghostly touch, even while I feared the real Touch from it. What if in certain cases Touch acted by itself, co-present with vision, yet not coalescing – then I should see the finger as at a distance, and yet feel a finger

19

touching which was nothing but it & yet was not it / the two senses cannot co-exist without a sense of causation / the *touch* must be the effect of that Finger, I see, yet it's not yet near to me, <and therefore it is not it; & yet it is it. Why,> it is it in an imaginary preduplication. N.B. there is a passage in the second Part of Wallenstein, expressing not explaining the same feeling – The Spirits of great Events Stride on before the events – it is in one of the last two or 3 Scenes.

How few would read this Note – nay, *any one?* / and not think the writer mad or drunk! [*CN* II 3215]

The richness and variety of Coleridge's notes on sleep and dreaming, as seen in the notebooks, is a subject in itself for an experienced analyst with the soul of a poet and a wide reading equal to Coleridge's own. No wonder no one has explored it. One can scarcely imagine what it was like to write or think like this about dreams at a time when dreams were treated in the context of prophecy, foreboding, tabus, and ghosts. Astonishingly prescient about what he called 'the afflictions of sleep,' Coleridge said, 'Every Dream has its scheme,' contrasting dream with delirium in this respect (*CN* V). What are the links with such feelings as fear, terror, and rage, he wonders (*CN* III 4046). The 'Dreamatis Personae are combined with *motives*, generally suggested by the Passions' (*CN* V). Again he compares dreams with nightmare and with reverie. He had asserted the dogma, he says, that 'the Forms & Feelings of sleep are *always* the reflections & confused Echoes of our waking Thoughts & Experiences' but now he wonders if this is so. He has also been curious about the link between bodily pain, a cramp, any physical sensation, and nightmares; he concludes that 'the Terror does not arise out of a painful Sensation but is itself a specific sensation' (*CN* III 4046). He asks, whence the weeping and self-pity in dreams? He is aware of sexual elements (*CN* II 2055, 2600). And he wonders why certain kinds of dreams of fear and anger regularly go back to school days and Christ's Hospital (*CN* II 2613). But there are about three hundred entries on dreams and sleep, in which the very questions he asks himself point to the slenderness of our knowledge of our inner life.

I turn here to some other kinds of self-examination, also typical. Many of us can recognize this one:

If one thought leads to another, so often does it blot out another – This I find, when having lain musing on my Sopha, a number of interesting Thoughts have suggested themselves, I conquer my bodily indolence & rise to record them in these books, alas! my only Confidants. – The first Thought leads me on indeed to new ones; but nothing but the faint memory of having had them remains of the others, which had been even more interesting to me. – I do not know, whether this be an idiosyncracy, a peculiar disease, of *my* particular memory – but so it is with *me* – My Thoughts crowd each other to death. [*CN* III 3342]

That was written in 1808 when Coleridge was thirty years old, and already, Hamlet-like, applying the word *disease* to himself.

Three years earlier he had jotted down an example of this form of forgetfulness:

... What is the right, the virtuous Feeling, and consequent action, when a man having long meditated & perceived a certain Truth finds another & a foreign Writer, who has handled the same with an approximation to the Truth, as he <had previously> conceived it? – Joy! – Let Truth make her Voice *audible*! While I was preparing the pen to write this remark, I lost the train of Thought which had led me to it. I meant to have asked something else, now forgotten: for the above answers itself – it needed no new answer, I trust, in my Heart. 14 April, 1805 – [*CN* II 2546]

In fact I suspect the 'train of Thought' he lost track of was in the observation immediately preceding on the page overleaf!

Saturday Night, April 14, 1805 – In looking at objects of Nature while I am thinking, as at yonder moon dim-glimmering thro' the dewy window-pane, I seem rather to be seeking, as it were *asking*, a symbolical language for something within me that already and forever exists, than observing any thing new. Even when that latter is the case, yet still I have always an obscure feeling as if that new phaenomenon were the dim Awaking of a forgotten or hidden Truth of my inner Nature / It is still interesting as a Word, a Symbol! It is Λογος, the Creator! <and the Evolver!> [*CN* II 2546]

The active participating response to the book of nature is both projective and receptive: inner and outer worlds come together in the Word, the Symbol. Perhaps the daring application of the word Logos to himself made him drop the subject, in fright.

He reflects on the nature of *habit* on which he had once proposed to write an essay:

Of *Habit* – O how miserable this makes me, not only as recalling an evil *habit*, but as recalling one of its consequences – what glorious, original Notions I had of this untreated of subject 5 years ago – & nothing done: - & I understand it less now by far, than I did then – All the dim Analoga of Habit in Inanimate forms [are] either the Effect of some actual alteration in the substance of the thing – ex. gr. an old Violin as giving a mellower sound than new wood – or act only defectively, as the rumple in a Leaf of long continuance – None of these seem even to give a decent *Simile* for the increase (almost indefinite) of *Power* by Practice in a vital Being – the muscular motions of a capital Performress on the Piano Forte, or (O bless the fair white arms of dear departed Laura Montague!) on the Pedal Harp – &c &c &c. – [*CN* III 3361]

(It would be cheating to spare you the comedy of some of Coleridge's sentimental illustrations.)

Clearly he knew he was blocked by his own emotions connected with this subject of habit. The introspective initiative is patently clear, but notice how it moves outwards, to the more objective general question of the physiology of habit – and how does practice increase *power* – even muscularly? If only he could understand – *and* apply that!

The sense of contradiction then, between the world within him and the world without, was there from earliest days and seems to have fostered a capacity for asking questions that went on developing throughout his life. Sometimes simply inquisitive, sometimes rebellious, spontaneous inquiry of all sorts was second nature to Coleridge; it brought some kind of focusing of the sensory, the mental, the physical, the personal restlessness. Nothing is too minute or trivial; nothing too fundamental or vast.

1. Feb. 1805. Friday. Malta. Of the Millions that use the Pen, how many (quere) understand the theory of this simple machine, the action of the Slit, Etc? – I confess, ridiculous as it must appear to those who do understand it, that I have not been able to answer the question off-hand to myself, having only this moment thought of it. [*CN* II 2423]

One cold damp Malta morning in January 1805 having just recorded that he has been appointed Public Secretary pro tem he reflects on the wood fire in his fireplace:

On a heap of glowing wood embers throw a quantity of large and small Chips and Shavings – & they will all quietly and moulderingly change into the substance of fire – but apply even the smallest Match with the faintest blue *flame* and tho' with a thousandfold less Heat it will set the whole instantly on flame. – A good Simile for sympathy of

23

a predisposed multitude with the courage of some Massaniello [a seventeenth-century Spanish demagogue who led a revolt] – but physically, what is the reason of this phaenomenon! that flame is ignited vapor says nothing till one knows what it is that ignites vapor. Can it be supposed that the tapering blue flame of a match or even of a bit of phosphorus is more intense† than that of a whole Hearth of glowing Embers? – Is not some business of affinity concerned here / the heat in the flame existing in a state of greater *repulsion* & therefore more eager to combine with bodies out of itself – [*CN* II 2409]

Then he puts a footnote to the word *intense*:† 'a bit of phosphorus is more intense than that of a whole Hearth of glowing Embers?' saying to himself, 'Yes! than equal space of embers.'

The physics of his answer may be dubious but the question is the thing. The phenomenon fascinated him first as a juxtaposition of opposites, then as a simile for mob psychology (the demagogue match and the mass of embers ready to be inflamed). But from there he takes off and pursues the subject of flame (the triangular symbol of his personal seal is among other things a flame symbol). 'What *is* inflammability?' had been a theme in Humphry Davy's first chemistry lectures in the Royal Institution in 1802. Here Coleridge's notebook question to himself comes with a touch of irony – the single little match and the whole bed of embers. What is the principle here, governing the relation between bodies? Affinity? Repulsion? Is the phrase, 'and therefore more *eager* to combine with bodies out of itself' merely an example of pathetic fallacy, or is it an unconscious personal metaphor? *Eager* is surely an emotive word.

This is one aspect of what I mean by suggesting that Coleridge's thinking is rooted in personal experience, the minutiae as well as the wider arcs. His curiosity arises from a combination of mental concentration, observation, and an inexplicable personal drive. The directions it takes are not necessarily personal; they may well be an escape from the personal, for much of that from childhood onwards was painful and introspective. Yet Coleridge's sense of isolation did not destroy him. It fostered creative activity.

It has more than once been said that among English poets Coleridge was the great poet of childhood, and of love. That Coleridge understood these out of pain rather than pleasure did not block the detachment necessary to articulate them. He is also the poet of loneliness, the emotional setting of many of his finest poems, including the greatest lyrical ballad of loneliness in the language. His lonely characters may be seen sharply in contrast with Wordsworth's solitaries – those much more self-possessed and harmonious Leech Gatherers and Solitary Reapers. Coleridge's Ancient Mariner and Christabel are sufferers, incomplete in their relation to life, searching for someone to talk to. Like their creator. Hence the dialogue, actual or implicit in so many of the poems. Hence the need (faute de mieux) to make the notebooks his confidants. Coleridge was lonely because he was a warmly gregarious man.

A line in quotation marks, buried in a notebook entry, gave me many a fruitless search. 'I am not a god that I should stand alone.' Finally after about two decades of hunting, up many blind alleys, it appeared in a Coleridge sale; he quoted it casually in a manuscript letter as from an unpublished poem *of his own*! His deep personal sense of the godlike and ungodlike in loneliness refined his insights, e.g. into Shakespeare's tragic heroes as they endure or do not endure their isolation; it is part of his painful critical sense of the imagination as creator. To be free to initiate it must be free enough to stand alone. He had no confidence that he himself could do so, yet it is, I believe, an overlooked nobility in Coleridge – his frailties are more obvious – that he was able so often to turn his personal loneliness to creative use. The poems, the literary criticism, the philosophy, all were wrenched out of a complex total experience. Failure to understand this is failure to come anywhere near the truth about Coleridge. To understand it makes most of the charges against him trivial. The basis of his strength seems to me to be his awareness of the difficulties of reconciling everywhere those opposites which he first met within himself.

In the second lecture I should like to look at some of the strange paths along which Coleridge's curiosity about and association with other minds took him, as for example his interest in imaginative originals like Behmen, Paracelsus, and Bruno. In the third lecture I shall say something more about his own poetic and philosophic imagination especially as it is exhibited in the notebook-keeper.

❧ LECTURE TWO ❧

❈❖❈ LECTURE TWO ❈❖❈

I N THE FIRST LECTURE I suggested that the circumstances of Coleridge's early life as he described them encouraged in him the constant questioning of the appearances of things, and a sense of conflict between inner and outer worlds. He became, as he said, an oddity, an unwilling solitary, against the grain of a sociable temper.

It is well known that he became also one of the most omnivorous of English readers, one with a taste for certain kinds of eccentrics. Or was it a taste and a search for something else? Coleridge was not altogether the literary Don Quixote he is sometimes made out to be. As his grandson Ernest Hartley Coleridge said, 'Coleridge for all his eccentricities was the sanest of mortals.'

I should like now to examine some examples of his curious reading and the various drives behind it which were more positive and logical than a mere taste for other social rejects – such obscure yet notorious rebels of earlier times as Jacob Behmen, and Bruno, and Paracelsus – and certain intellectual odd-men-out in his own day.

Coleridge approached other independent minds keenly alive to their loneliness and courage, and with immense respect for them. In November 1803, a soul-destroying time of self-flagellation, he wrote in Notebook 21:

With a deep groan from the Innermost of my Heart, in the feeling of self-humiliation, & a lively sense of my own weakness, & the distraction of my mind, which is indeed 'always doing something else,' I yet write down the names of the Works that I have planned, in the order in which I wish to execute them, with a fervent prayer that I may build up in my Being enough of manly Strength & Perseverence to do one thing at a time – [*CN* I 1646]

There follows a list of vast works; the first was on 'Man, and the probable Destiny of the Human Race.' The ninth and tenth were to be on 'Revolutionary Minds, Thomas Aquinas, Scotus, Luther, [Richard] Baxter... Socinus, G. Fox... Giordano Bruno, Jacob Boehmen, Spinoza.' That resolution is succeeded in the notebook by another entry:

It has been long my sincere wish, & (for that all our Habits partake of human Frailty) my *pride*, to try to understand, in myself, & to make intelligible to others, how great men may err *wildly*, yet not be mad – that all opinions that can be understood & are not contrad[ictory] in terms have more to be said for them than Bigots & Pedants & Sciolists suppose. [*CN* I 1647]

'How great men may err wildly, yet not be mad.' Though he did not think of himself as a great man – ('I have a sense of power without strength' was a sincere and repeated confession) – he did know what it was to 'err wildly yet not be mad,' at least not so mad as brother George chose to think him. He also knew that imagination was in his scheme of things a concomitant of genius, but so often suspected of madness that a man of imagination had to be brave also. Of his 'Revolutionary Minds' it is hard to say whether it was their imagination or their temerity he admired most. Coleridge was an early appreciator of the historical fact that the imagination is sometimes prophetic, seizing intuitively on truths that science later, with mightier accumulations of other kinds of evidence, labours to bring forth.

One of his earliest heroes was Jacob Böhme or Behmen, the German theosophist shoemaker (1575-1624) whose works in four large quarto volumes were published in English translation about the time of Coleridge's birth. They were heavily annotated by Coleridge at several readings till nearly the end of his life; but long before he obtained them and while he was still a schoolboy, he read or rather he said, 'conjured over' (a nice distinction) Behmen's *Aurora* – the earliest and one of the more difficult of Behmen's visionary works.

No doubt part of the early attraction was Behmen's personal misfortunes. Dismissed from his shoemaking shop because of the uncontrolled intensity of his mystical experiences and heterodox teachings, he became a wandering journeyman and although quite uneducated was attacked by the orthodox authorities with a vigour and ruthlessness as difficult to comprehend as the writings that provoked them. But to a youth like Coleridge, already given to inner exploration, and therefore with some sense of a world of fantasy and symbol, Behmen set forth, often in highly paradoxical aphorisms, a mystical vision of the forces behind the life of the senses. His counsel was no doubt comforting and pacifying to a precocious adolescent troubled by his own conflicts over the discrepancies between outer and inner realities. Concentrate on the inward, Behmen urged, 'learn to distinguish between the Thing, and that which is only an image thereof, between the sovereignty which is substantial and in the inward ground of Nature, and that which is imaginary and in outward form of semblance; between that which is properly angelical, and that which is no more than bestial.'[1]

The passage is too clear to be typical of Behmen, whose confused, interminable, and intensely pious arguments are baffling, to say the least, to the point of despair; yet Isaac Newton, and William Blake, and Coleridge were among those who respected him. Coleridge's marginalia helped me to grasp that Behmen viewed the life of man and the whole cosmos in one and the same pattern. Hence the sudden leaps of thought, from one plane to another, the curious allegorical way of writing, using strange terms and terms with more than

1 *Of the Supersensual Life* Dialogue I

31

one meaning, e.g. Salitter (Saltpetre), for the 'divine Powers' and also for Gravitation. Behmen saw the universal struggle, physical in the universe and moral in man, as a struggle between the conflicting forces of light and darkness, and described these forces variously in both human and cosmic terms: expansion and contraction, centrifugal and centripetal, repulsion and attraction, the astringent quality and the sweet quality, the destructive and the constructive, humility and pride, anguish and joy. For Behmen God is the Abyss, the Urgrund, of Nature and Man, something like Spinoza's *substantia*, yet unlike 'substance' in being a fountain of light. Behmen saw most of society as living on the circumference of reality, and the individual soul as a spark of the divine in need of realizing its inborn longing for 'the central Fire.' Man may grow towards the centre, he thought, or away from centre to the mere appearance of life. Each soul's task is to pursue self-knowledge in order to rejoin the original Fire. It is the function of maturing knowledge and religious growth to direct him towards the centre from which he sprang, so that the Fire of anguish and desire becomes, through the fulfilment of divine longing, the Light of love.

Coleridge conceded that sometimes he found Behmen incomprehensible, also pantheistic in his apparent transposing of God and the World or Nature; the marginalia on the Behmen volumes are often mystified or critical. Behmen's works in what is commonly known as Law's edition are difficult, as all mystical writings are to the novice, but these are made a thousand times more so by Behmen's unorganized profusion of imagery, often in a private tortuous language. (*Anguish*, one of his favourite words, describes the state of mind of any ordinary reader.) Yet Coleridge while still a schoolboy was fascinated enough by Behmen's desperate attempts to enunciate his troubled insights into the conflicts in the human condition to fight his way through.

It would be folly in a paragraph or two, even if one felt more secure than I do in one's understanding of Behmen, to elucidate fully the ramifications of his thought. In any case, it is not Behmen's particular views we are concerned with here, but rather Coleridge's analysis of a religious philosopher, a theosophist, two hundred years before him. The main statement is in the eleventh of *The Philosophical Lectures* (329-31). Having referred to Behmen's 'delusions, from want of all intellectual discipline' and from 'ignorance of rational psychology,' the latter 'in common with the most learned theologians of his age,' Coleridge says,

He was indeed a stupendous human being. Had he received the discipline of education, above all had he possessed the knowledge which would have guarded him against his own delusions, I scarcely know whether we should have had reason to attribute greater genius even to Plato himself. When I consider that this ignorant man by the result of his own meditations presented the Newtonian system [by anticipation] in a clearness which it certainly had never before appeared in, not even to Copernicus himself, or to the learned Bruno [Coleridge refers to what looks like some concept of universal gravitation in Behmen]; when I trace in him the love of action and that constant sense of the truth that all nature is in a perpetual evolution, that two great powers are for ever working, manifesting themselves alike in the apparently inadequate and inanimated, and in intellectual nature, (namely the powers by which each particular endeavours to detach itself from nature and the counteracting powers by which nature is still bringing back each of her creatures into itself – this led him assuredly into anticipations and views of truth which will detract from many modern discoveries some part, at least, of their originality); but above all that spirit of love which runs through him; that dread of contempt; that belief that the potential works in us even as the actual is working on us, and that not only man but every creature contains in itself a higher being, ...

He then refers to Behmen's tendency to pantheism.

From this I cannot excuse Behmen's writings, any more than I can praise or attempt or pretend to understand many of the strange fancies by which he has represented his truths. Sometimes indeed one can guess at the meaning; sometimes it is utter darkness. And altogether he represents a great mirror, but placed in the shade; all the objects of nature seem to pass by, but they are reflected in shadow and dimly, but now and then a light passes along and the mirror in the shade flashes...

Coleridge was willing to work for his gains from a difficult writer. He found in Behmen what he was searching for, some liberation from the 'fixities and definites' of the late eighteenth-century applications of Newtonian physics and Lockian psychology which had prevailed in his undergraduate days. It delighted Coleridge to read 'that all nature is in a perpetual evolution, that two great powers are forever working' – 'the belief that the potential works in us' – 'above all the Spirit of love.' The universe was therefore not static, but in process, and man was not a despairing cog in the Newtonian machine. Therefore all that is, is not necessarily right, but changing, and man participates actively, not passively, and by imagination and love. God was not arbitrary, but continually creating the universe out of material and spiritual force, a fountain of fire, energy, and light. (The fountain was a highly integrating image in Coleridge's poems, a central symbol for a dynamic, unifying energy; it was central to all his thinking.) Perhaps the most radical theme of all in Behmen and the most satisfying to Coleridge was the daring – or naive – or at any rate unapologetic – assumption of the naturalness of the conjunction of thought and feeling. On that assumption Coleridge's case for the potency of imagination was built.

In the summer of 1801 Coleridge was reading Henry More's *Brief Discourse of Enthusiasm* in which More gave what he snobbishly called 'divers odd conceits out of several "Theosophists and Chymists"' without naming the authors. Coleridge identified one of them as Jacob Behmen, though More's paraphrase of Behmen's *Aurora* was somewhat rough and casual. More also referred to Paracelsus sneeringly through five sections, whereupon Coleridge at once made a note, to get hold of Paracelsus:

Behmen's opinion – That all is God's self – that a man's self is God if he live holily – that the Waters of this World are mad – / likewise endeavour to get Paracelsus de Meteoris, his Scientia Astronom[ica], & his de natura rerum. [*CN* I 1000 E]

He did see Paracelsus, the three-volume Geneva edition of 1658; his friend J.H. Green's copy is now in the library of the Royal College of Physicians and Surgeons. Which works did he read? One wonders. Although Paracelsus (1493-1541) is sometimes called the Martin Luther of medicine, reports are contradictory, many of them from hostile contemporaries to whom his radical ideas constituted a threat. It is clear that he offered Coleridge some grounds for identification, perhaps also for envious contrast, and yet it is also clear that Paracelsus was a bold, contentious, arrogant fellow. (The name Paracelsus he gave to himself, i.e. 'greater than – Celsus.') John Donne, among others, attributed his legendary medical powers to a Faust-like communication with the Devil. He was rough, of no academic standing, yet all the time aggressively proposing experiments and theories to upset the conventional professionals who refused to question Aristotle's ipse dixits. He attacked and indeed was instrumental in destroying as a medical theory the notion of the 'humours,' and insisted on inquiring into specific diseases and specific cures. And he had some astonishing good luck as a practitioner, confounding the greybeards. He gave one of the first clinical descriptions of syphilis, suggesting a biochemical cure, with mercury. Full of contradictions, at the same time as he was insisting on treatment of the human organism as a whole, and stressing the mind of the patient as a necessary part of it, the man also was going in for alchemy and astrology, and claiming intimacy with occult forces. Attacking contemporary medical bigotry, fraud, and ignorance, he yet pretended to communications of his own with superior powers – a familiar enough defence mechanism. Boerhaave described him, according to Coleridge, 'as a great, anomalous, unaccountable fellow' [*CN* III 4414].

In the *Notebooks* the first direct quotation from Paracelsus is from the *Paragranum*, said to be the most savage attack on doctors ever written. It was his most brutal (and central) work, the one in which he destroyed the theory of 'the humours,' inventing instead his new physiological hypotheses about the human body as an independent organic whole. In the notebook entry Coleridge quoted in the Latin the famous passage in which Paracelsus – who advocated natural cures – perversely said, 'Nature itself is a disease.' Coleridge versified his own grim personal extrapolation:

> Ills from without extrinsic Balms may heal,
> Oft cur'd & wounded by the self-same Steel –
> But us what remedy can heal or cure,
> Whose very nature is our worst disease. [*CN* III 3616]

A few pages later in the same notebook Coleridge made notes on more passages from the *Paragranum*, including the preface by Bitisky defending Paracelsus against charges of 'obscurity' and of unnecessarily coining new terms – charges all too familiar to Coleridge himself. E.g. one of the new words coined by Paracelsus (and then used by Behmen) was of central interest to Coleridge, the word *Archeus*, the idea of a seminal Reason or Logos, a vital principle. He took from Paracelsus a quotation he applied later on to himself:

What does it matter to me whether they follow or pursue me? I shall not try to force them. I shall, however, expose them, because they altogether abound in frauds and impostures and h͞av͞e͞ no other foundation than that which arises from the itch for the applause of the mob and from ignorance. Whoever is faithful and honest to his own heart, and whoever in practice tries to imitate nature in art, will not avoid me or turn away. [*CN* III 3660 and n]

Coleridge's most sustained statement about Paracelsus is found in a note in the margins of Fuller's *Holy State* (Bk II ch 3) on Fuller's Life of Paracelsus. As usual, enthusiasm is tempered with but not damped by critical judgement:

It is matter of regret with me, that Fuller (whose wit alike in quantity, quality and perspicuity surpassing that of the wittiest in a witty Age, ... had not looked thro' the two Latin Folios of Paracelsus's Works. It is not to be doubted, that a rich and delightful Article would have been the result. / For who like Fuller, could have brought out, and set forth, this singular Compound of true philosophic Genius with the morals of a Quack and the manners of a King of the Gypsies? Nevertheless, Paracelsus belonged to his Age, viz. the Dawn of Experimental Science; and a well-written Critique on his Life & Writings would present thro' the magnifying glass of a Caricature the distinguishing features of the Helmonts, Kircher, in short, of the host of Naturalists of the 16th Century – / ... [He continues, on the subject of Alchemy]: ... N.b. The Potential (= Λογος Θεανθρωπος), the ground of the Prophetic, directed the first *Thinkers* (= Mystæ) to the metallic bodies, as the Key of all natural Science. The *then* Actual blended with this instinct all the fancies, and fond desires, and false *perspective*, of the Childhood of Intellect. The *essence* was truth, the *form* was folly: and this is the definition of Alchemy. – Nevertheless, the very terms bear witness to the veracity of the original Instinct / The World of Sensible Experience cannot be more luminously divided than into the modifying powers, το αλλον – that which *differences*, makes this *other* than that: and the μετ' αλλον, that which is beyond or deeper than modification. Metallon is strictly 'the *Base* of the Mode:' and such have the Metals been determined to be by modern Chemistry. – And what are now the great problems of Chemistry? The difference of the Metals themselves, their origin, the causes of their locations, of their co-existence in the same ore (ex. gr. of Iridium, Osmium, Palladium, Rhodium, and Iron with Platinum). – Were these problems solved, the results who dare limit? ...

And the annotation on Fuller's *Life* ends with:

The Light was for the greater part suffocated, and the rest fantastically refracted; but still it was Light struggling in the darkness. And I am persuaded, that to the full triumph of Science, it will be necessary that Nature should be commanded more *spiritually* than hitherto – i.e. more directly in the power of THE WILL.

Is there not a modern ring to this? Are physicists, chemists, ecologists, and all the rest of us, not now talking about the 'moral responsibilities' of science?

It is evident that Coleridge's admiration for Paracelsus was far from idolatrous, but it is also clear that the attractions of Paracelsus's subject and his originality were such as to draw Coleridge into his folio volumes to try to understand the thinking of this wild, rude, lonely, original man, 'a pilgrim all my life,' Paracelsus said, 'alone and a stranger feeling alien,' whose aggressions produced the stormy works attacking his whole profession; and who yet said, 'the ground of all medicine is love.'

Paracelsus next to Behmen must be one of the more unclear of writers. He was unclear to himself. That Coleridge appears to have understood the central positions through the wild turmoil of physiology, prophecy, alchemical and astrological muddle, out of the chinks in which glimmer some lights from a primitive biochemistry and psychology, all in a rough Swiss-German dialect or less than elegant Latin, is a sign of Coleridge's persistence and skills as a reader, rather than of Paracelsian lucidity. The most fundamental Paracelsian discovery and hyphothesis was that diseases are both visible and invisible. This Coleridge understood better than most.

He was not concerned to establish the correctness of Paracelsian medicine. Undoubtedly the fascinating thing about Paracelsus was his coarse and ruthless scepticism about the prevailing assumptions of his time. This provoked his unremitting search for 'forces' within man and within nature, forces within the microcosmos and the macrocosmos alike to be comprehended as one 'Archeus,' one set of laws, thus to free man from the mental bondage of hidebound quackery and the arbitrariness of ignorant men with power. It was the search for law, laws of mind and laws of nature, and the human processes behind discovery of them that made Paracelsus interesting to Coleridge, not Paracelsus's conclusions.[2] The attempted integration of man and nature was pursued with less piety and more science, and more ferocity in this case than in Behmen's, but a common denominator was there for Coleridge.

2 In Southey's *Omniana* (1812) 1216 Coleridge wrote: 'Paracelsus was a braggart and a quack; so was Cardan, but it was their merits, and not their follies, which drew upon them that torrent of detractions and calumny.'

Giordano Bruno (1548-1600) was better known in Coleridge's time for his stubborn martyrdom at the stake than for his writings. It was Bruno the heretical astronomer-philosopher, poet and defiant satirist of complacent academia, in whom Coleridge was interested. Curiously he did not discuss at length the Bruno of the art of memory, so learnedly elucidated by Frances Yates. Bruno's works – about twenty-six are known by title, of which Coleridge saw at least six[3] – were very scarce and thought to be nonsense. In Bruno's defence, Coleridge complained that they were often full of what seemed 'impenetrable obscurity, in which Bruno shares one and the same fate with Plato, Aristotle, Kant, and in truth with every great discoverer and benefactor of the human race; excepting only when the discoveries have been capable of being rendered palpable to the outward senses.'[4]

Bruno's imaginative comprehension of an infinity of worlds, each impelled in its own motion by its own nature and yet part of an infinite whole, cast doubt on the old Aristotelian series of concentric spheres with the earth fixed in the middle, and even on the Copernican modification of the annual rotation of the earth around the sun and the daily rotation on its axis. Bruno saw that Copernicus had in fact introduced a completely new cosmology. Bruno envisaged a vast organic cosmos in which all phenomena in space and time, material and spiritual, were related. It was certainly a vision too big for

3 See *CN* II 2264 and *Friend* (*CC*) I 118.
4 'Magnanimity': *Omniana* § 129. The little essay continues by referring disparagingly to ' "our sober judicious critics", the men of "sound common sense", i.e. of those snails in intellect who wear their eyes at the tips of their feelers, and cannot even see unless they at the same time *touch* – When these finger-philosophers affirm that Plato, Bruno, &c must have been "*out of their senses*", the just and proper retort is "Gentlemen! it is still worse with you! You have *lost your reason*!" '

most minds. Earth was no longer a special creation, hence the charge of heresy. And what of the application of cosmic infinity to human life? This was not pressed home by Bruno, so far as I have been able to read him, but the relativist implications did not escape a Coleridge.

Coleridge must have found a fellow-feeling in Bruno's charming anecdote in the poem, *De Immenso*, of how as a child, living in Nola in Italy, on the slopes of Mt Cicada and thus much aware of that same 'Vast' that Coleridge came to know in Ottery St Mary, he too learned the disparity between appearance and reality, or as he said, 'how distance changes the face of things.' He tells of how when he was a child Mt Cicada used to speak to him of the rival beauty of the mountain opposite, Mt Vesuvius. So he walked over and climbed Vesuvius which also spoke to him, of the darkness and dreariness of its opposite – Mt Cicada. But the young Bruno informed Vesuvius that such was exactly its own appearance from Cicada, and that really Cicada was just as beautiful. Bruno says of himself and this fantasy, 'Thus did they first teach the lad to doubt.' And we might add, to philosophize.

From *De Immenso*, the first long quotations in the *Notebooks* in the original Latin were taken in 1801, the first excerpt being an example of Bruno's well-known truculence which Coleridge liked to quote and sometimes applied to himself: 'Pay particular attention, I beseech you, to these things (i.e. the new view of the cosmos as infinite): in that way you may understand me, a person who may perhaps seem mad – or at least see why I am mad' (*CN* I 927); Coleridge used it in his periodical, *The Friend*, in defence of his attacks on the lamentable state of public taste and knowledge in 1809. There he glossed Bruno: 'What I feel deeply, freely will I utter. Truth is not Detraction: and assuredly we do not hate him to whom we tell the Truth. But with whomsoever we play the Deceiver and Flatterer, him at the bottom we despise.'[5]

There are further selections (eight pages of Latin) copied out by hand from *De Immenso* with Coleridge's running comments; it is characteristic of what goes on in the notebooks.

First Coleridge leapt into the middle of the work, extracting the piece just quoted (*CN* I 927). He then added: 'Bruno, p. 524, 525, 528 *De Univ[erso] et Innum[erabilis]* speaks familiarly of the circulation of the Blood – & not only of the Circulatio minor discovered by Servetus,' and he referred to the relevant passages. (This material was later used by Coleridge in an article on 'The circulation of the Blood' in Southey's catch-all *Omniana* of 1812, § 122.)

Perhaps it was the next day or soon after that Coleridge decided to begin a more systematic study of Bruno and took a fresh page: 'Monday, April. 1801. – and Tuesday, read two Works of Giordano Bruno, printed in one book with one title-page,' and he gives in full the long titles of two works *De Monade, Numero, et Figurâ*, and *De Immenso* with the names of the Frankfurt printers and the date, 1591. (Many of Bruno's works had been given deceptive imprints for the safety of the printers, otherwise like Bruno, open to charges of heresy.) Coleridge described the physical volume, and commented:

Then the Work 'De Monade, Numero et Figurâ, secretioris nempe Physicae, Mathematicae, & Metaphysicae elementa' commences – which as well as the 8 books de Innumer.&c is a Poem in latin Hexameters, divided (each Book) into Chapters, & to each Chapter is affixed a prose Commentary. If the 5 books de Minimo, &c to which this Book is consequent, are of the same character, I lost nothing in not having it. The work de Monade. – It was far too numeral, lineal, & pythagorean for my Comprehension – it read very much like Thomas Taylor & Proclus &c. I by no means think it certain that there is no meaning in these Works, nor do I presume even to suppose, that the meaning is of no value – / but it is <till I understand a man's Ignorance, I presume myself ignorant of his understanding> for others, at present, not for me – Sir P. Sidney, & Fulk Greville shut the doors at their philos. conferences with Bruno – if his Conversation resembled this Book, I should have thought, he would [have] talked with a trumpet. [*CN* I 928]

'The poem, <& Commentaries,> de Immenso et Innumerabili is of a different character – ' he said, excerpting poetic passages in which Bruno seeks (to quote him in Coleridge's translation) 'the splendor, the interfusion, and communication of the Divinity and of Nature' and contemplates

the Host of Stars, of Worlds and their guardian Deities, numbers without number, each in its appointed sphere, singing together, and dancing in adoration of the One Most High. Thus from the perpetual, immense, and innumerable goings on of the visible world, that sempiternal and absolutely infinite Majesty is intellectually beheld ... Thence was man entitled by Trismegistus, 'the great Miracle', inasmuch as he has been made capable of entering into union with God, as if he were himself a divine nature; tries to *become* all things, even as in God all things *are*; and in limitless progression of limited States of being, urges onward to the ultimate aim, even as God is simultaneously infinite, and everywere All! [*CN* I 928n]

Coleridge, like the Church, was able to discern the scientific thought behind the poetic language, but, whereas Coleridge was excited and delighted, the Church charged such poetry with dangerous pantheism and burned Bruno as a heretic for his refusal to retract.

In his *Essay on Man* Cassirer makes a useful statement about the significance of Bruno in his time:

... In Stoic philosophy and in Christian theology man was described as the end of the universe. Both doctrines are convinced that there is a general providence ruling over the world and the destiny of man. This concept is one of the basic presuppositions of Stoic and Christian thought. All this is suddenly called into question by the new cosmology. Man's claim to being the center of the universe has lost its foundation. Man is placed in an infinite space in which his being seems to be a single and vanishing point. He is surrounded by a mute universe, by a world that is silent to his religious feelings and to his deepest moral demands ... Modern philosophy and modern science had to accept the challenge contained in these words. They had to prove that the new cosmology, far from enfeebling or obstructing the power of human reason, establishes and confirms this power ... to turn the apparent curse of the new cosmology into a blessing. Giordano Bruno was the first thinker to enter upon this path, which in a sense became the path of all modern metaphysics. What is characteristic of the philosophy of Giordano Bruno is that here the term 'infinity' changes its meaning. In Greek classical thought infinity is a negative concept. The infinite is the boundless or indeterminate ... In Bruno's doctrine infinity no longer means a mere negation or limitation. On the contrary, it means the immeasurable and inexhaustible abundance of reality and the unrestricted power of the human intellect. It is in this sense that Bruno understands and interprets the Copernican doctrine. This doctrine, according to Bruno, was the first and decisive step toward man's self-liberation. Man no longer lives in the world as a prisoner enclosed within the narrow walls of a finite physical universe. He can traverse the air and break through all the imaginary boundaries of the celestial spheres which have been erected by a false metaphysics and cosmology. The infinite universe sets no limits to human reason. The human intellect becomes aware of its own infinity through measuring its powers by the infinite universe.[6]

6 Ernst Cassirer *An Essay on Man: An Introduction to a Philosophy of Human Culture* (1953) 32-3

Coleridge defended Bruno as 'a vigorous mind struggling after truth, amid many prejudices';[7] he even wondered whether he shouldn't try to borrow from Malta, Bruno's work on Logic where he had seen the one copy he knew of. For what purpose? It is typical of Coleridge's dynamic relation to a thinker, regardless of period. He felt Bruno's sixteenth-century logic was just what was needed to prick the bubble of loose complacent nineteenth-century optimism about electricity. The voltaic pile, discovered in 1799 (hard upon the *Lyrical Ballads* but creating considerably more noise) made electricity a subject in fashionable drawing rooms. Everything was to be explained, everything to be solved by it. Coleridge, who read the latest scientific journals and attended many of the lectures of Davy, Brande, and others, at the Royal Institution, was horrified by all the lax talk and sheer stupid fashionableness:

I do not like that presumptuous Philosophy which in its rage of explanation allows no xyz, no symbol representative of the vast Terra Incognita of Knowlege, for the Facts and Agencies of Mind and matter reserved for future Explorers / while the ultimate grounds of all must remain inexplorable or Man must cease to be progressive. Our Ignorance with all the intermediates of obscurity is the *condition* of our ever-increasing Knowlege. Consider for a moment the multitude and the importances of the phænomena now universally referred to electric agency – not to mention those now explained by the electro-chemical combination of the ponderable portion of oxygen Gas with metallic bases, or with hydrogen ... Having made a numeration-table of these Phænomena, then consult the Works of those Physiologists who flourished & uttered oracles before the discovery of Electricity. Their several explanations will furnish a Lesson not only of modesty but of Logic – For, doubtless, by a more

7 *Friend (CC)* II 81-2

watchful, and austere, as well as more modest & for that cause *anticipative*, Logic, the false part of these explanations might even then have been detected – & such explanations given, as would have preserved our existing quantum of knowlege pure from positive error, by avowedly including our ignorance in our knowlege, under a common Symbol. Thus in the old explanation of Thunder & Lightning, that it was Fire by the *dashing together* of Clouds – Here was *presumption* / Had they been contented to say, that clouds contained Fire in a latent form, which under given circumstances passed from one to the other; but that these circumstances, that is, that the *law* of Fire as contained in Vapors, remained to be discovered – all would have been right – and Fire would have been a fair generic term, or Symbol, which thus limited would have represented as in a process of Algebra, that particular species of Fire, which in the conclusion would have come out as Electricity. [*CN* III 3825]

He goes on to complain that people are too eager to explain everything:

... the whole explanation must be *seized* from the scanty possessions *behind* us, not *borrowed* from the vast tract *before* us – and because the former pigmy Domain contained the fact of Fire generated by collision, as of Flint & Steel, or by friction, as of the Wheel & Axle, therefore two *mists* in the air must be *dashed* against each other, or *rubbed* together. [*CN* III 3825]

The physical picture of collision, or friction, has easily usurped the place of real explanation; there is more of all this, but the entry ends:

... I exceedingly wish, I could procure from Malta the Logica Venatrix of Giord. Bruno.

The plan was fantastic in wartime (the date was 1810 and the Mediterranean convoys were anything but safe), but so *exceedingly* did he wish it he thought of applying to Lord Mulgrave (First Lord of the Admiralty), or to the Prime Minister! How can one *not* love Coleridge?

But this Coleridge, the passionate inquirer, is sceptical too. He is asking, what is the truth in all this application of the principles of electricity and what are those principles in reality? How much is assumption, how much picture-language, how much the overweening desire for one simple explanation for everything? Get at it by scrutinizing the thought processes behind it first. It was Coleridge's blinding realism out of his own experience to be able to see and describe and know the difference between things observed and things imagined. He will not be taken in either by the 'fashion' for electricity, or by reactionary authority's distaste for visionaries; visionaries just *may* have glimpses of what it lay ahead of their time to discover. The principle was the same as with Behmen, though Bruno was immensely learned whereas Behmen was uneducated. But Coleridge will take immense trouble to understand both.

If his interest in radical thinkers had been merely a sympathy for odd characters or heroic martyrs of the past, or brilliant individuals ahead of their time, it would give us an impression of his subjective choices in his world, and also some impressions of his sense of human history and some important actors in it. But the penetration is somewhat deeper than that.

In the same lecture quoted before, the eleventh of his *Philosophical Lectures*, Coleridge made a modern complaint about the strait-laced conventionality of scientists and philosophers (the passage is quoted in part by Loren Eiseley in *The Firmament of Time*):

Whoever is acquainted with the history of philosophy during the last two or three centuries, cannot but admit, that there appears to have existed a sort of secret and tacit compact among the learned, not to pass beyond a certain limit in speculative science. The privilege of free thought, so highly extolled, has at no time been held valid in actual practice, except within this limit; and not a single stride beyond it has ever been ventured without bringing obloquy on the transgressor ... [We can all think of today's examples.] Therefore the true depth of science, and the penetration to the inmost centre from which all the lines of knowledge diverge to their ever distant circumference, was abandoned to the illiterate and the simple [like Behmen], whom unstilled yearning, and an original ebulliency of spirit had urged to the investigation of the indwelling and living ground of all things. These then, because their names had never been enrolled in the guilds of the learned, were persecuted by the registered liverymen as interlopers on their rights and privileges. All without distinction were branded as fanatics and phantasts ... [such a man's] meditations are almost inevitably employed on the eternal or the everlasting, for 'the world is not his friend nor the world's law.' [*PL* 327-9]

We are back to the conflict between appearance and reality again, and Coleridge's distrust of the 'mere Facts' men over against the metaphysicians, of the professionals as against the imaginative amateurs. One may safely conclude that Coleridge chose his intellectual heroes[8] and allies, if Behmen, Paracelsus, and Bruno are a fair cross-section, for their daring, their doubting, and for the general snobbish and frightened neglect of their magnitude. He saw the same phenomenon in his own day, when his interest was stirred by

8 He himself named them, among others better known: Lessing, Schiller, Kant, Sidney, Shakespeare, Milton, Dante, Ariosto, Pascal, inter alios.

such notoriously unacceptable types as Mesmer, or Spurzheim. One could name many others, but I should like to refer briefly to these, chiefly to call attention to the common denominator in Coleridge's responses.

How much is it necessary at this time of day to describe Mesmer or mesmerism – the sort of subject we all know about, yet perhaps don't really know?

Mesmer, who died in 1815, practised a pseudo-hypnotism named after him – alternatively called 'animal magnetism.' He had first been an astrologer, and seems to have had some sort of fixation on the concept of cosmic magnetism and imponderable influences. He practised in Paris for about thirty years, and attracted many followers in and outside the medical profession, both in France and in Germany. The English generally regarded him with stolid (or solid, as you will) disbelief, and it is indeed difficult to imagine Londoners sitting, in seance-like sessions, as the Parisians did, holding hands in a circle around a cauldron full of some witches' brew while Mesmer, in magician's robes, floated among them, gesturing, touching, fixing with his glittering eye this or that hysterical patient. Scandalous stories mounted to the point where the French government asked Benjamin Franklin and other scientists to investigate. The resulting report was inconclusive as to the charlatanism, accrediting some of the facts and entirely repudiating Mesmer's theories of magnetic fluids, but leaving it possible to think that Mesmer was a genuine mystic who believed in his personal magnetic powers over diseased persons.

Coleridge did not know Mesmer; his first acquaintance with the writings of mesmerists seems to have been through C.A. Kluge's survey *Versuch einer Darstellung des animalischen Magnetismus, als Heilmittel* (1815) and for the next decade he read widely in the German literature on the subject.

There was no doubt a personal interest in the question whether in certain somatose conditions, hypnotic states of a sort, one person could influence another. On the front fly-leaf of Kluge Coleridge wrote:

Allowing the least possible to Fancy and Exaggeration, I can yet find nothing in the Cases collected by Dr. Kluge that requires any other conclusion but this – that under certain conditions one human Being may so act on the body as well as on the mind of another – as to produce a morbid sleep, from which the Brain awakes, while the organs of sense remain in stupor. I speak exclusively of the *intellectual* phaenomena of An[imal] Mag[netism]. That the same *vis ab extra* may act medically, there is no reason to doubt – any more than of the effects of opium. Thus the *modus agendi* in the first instance, the instrument thro' which the Magnetiser operates, is the only mystery: and on this neither Kluge nor any of his Predecessors have thrown a ray of Light. [*IS* § 32]

So 'Magnetism' may act medically – rather like opium. Was Coleridge's burning question whether an addict could be treated? In a manuscript fragment in the British Museum, probably intended for an article on animal magnetism, he wrote: 'Whence the contemptuous rejection of animal magnetism before and without examination?' Going on to reduce the hubbub to fundamentals,

... The only *position* ... asserted by Magnetists as Magnetists independent of all particular theory, or explanation) ... is, that the will or ... the *vis vitae* of Man is not confined in its operations to the Organic Body, in which it appears to be seated; but under certain previously defined Conditions of distance and position, and above all of the relation of the Patient to the Agent and of the Agent to the Patient, is capable of acting and producing certain pre-defined Effects on the living human bodies external to it.

Coleridge goes into particulars of mesmeric treatments in some detail, and concludes that Mesmer gave honest value for money, and was the victim of incomplete and biased evidence and gossip.

For myself, I shall even say – I will try it when I have the opportunity, myself – I will endeavour to see it tried by others, when I can – and till then I will be neutral – S.T. Coleridge, July 8th, 1817. [*IS* § 30]

Coleridge's attitude to mesmerism oscillated between pros and cons; he was as quick to spot quacks as the next one, and did not spare them. The interesting thing is that in the teeth of a great deal of popular mockery of it, he insisted on pursuing seriously a subject so closely related to obscure subterranean bodily and mental processes, an area in which even his friends were ignorant and prejudiced, as he well knew from personal experience.

Spurzheim (1776-1832) was another contemporary medical wild man about whom Coleridge's views were also wobbly, though on his general philosophical principles Coleridge could hardly support so physical a basis for mind as Spurzheim's theories implied. Spurzheim astonished the world by claiming to be able to describe a person's abilities and moral character by measuring the size, shape, and convolutions of his skull. But the fact that Abernethy was favourably impressed with Spurzheim's dissection and anatomy of the brain must have given Coleridge pause.

His first note (*CN* III 4269) on Spurzheim's *Physiognomical System* was derogatory of the whole work, its language, logic, and taste, but two years later a notebook entry begins:

August, 1817. I have since discovered that poor Spurzheim entrusted his Mss to a Scotch Man, a Murray I believe – & that no fair conception can be formed from the Book either of the System as presented in Spurzheim's Lectures, or of the Man, of whom all without exception who have known him, speak of with love and honor – Spurzheim is a true man, und ein biederer Teut[s]cher. – He has been driven out of the Kingdom to Paris by the malignity and malignant ignorance of Scotchmen / One Gordon and the Edingburgh Review – At present I think that Spurzheim is beyond all comparison the greatest Physiognomist that has ever appeared – that his intellectual γνωμονες or indices have stood the test of application to an astonishing number of Instances with a most imposing coincidence – of the moral Indices I have not the same favorable impression – and his Theory, which is perfectly separable from his Empeiria, I cannot bring into any consistency of meaning. [*CN* III 4355]

Spurzheim's examination of Coleridge's bumps led to an amusing P.S. in a letter to his friend Green in which he referred to 'the little less than idiocy of that same faculty of Locality, the size, prominence, and unusual development of the significant Bump-organ of which attracted the notice and excited the admiration of Professor *Spur*zheim, who consoled me therewith for the want, or evanescence, of the Organ of Ideality or Imagination.'[9]

Coleridge continued for some years to read Spurzheim's announcements of discoveries about the brain, as late notebook entries show, and to poke fun or disagree but always to be informed about the controversies, and to distrust the clack against Spurzheim, because, as he had said,

... were it only for the undoubted splendor and originality of his & Gall's Anatomical Discoveries as to the structure of the Brain – the clear Light thrown on the true state of the Brain in Hydrokephalos – he ought to have been answered, where answerable, with honor

9 *IS* § 27 n

& quiet detail of logical objections. One thing seems plain / that even if his System be true, it must constitute a *profession* – & why not? Is it not so with Medicine? Every man of Talent can learn from books the theory of Medicine; but from practical experience of his own must he acquire the power of safely applying it. [*CN* III 4355]

It is now recognized that Spurzheim, for all his extravagances, did imperfectly discover some true facts about the brain, e.g. that it is not just a pulpy mass, but fibrous, and that his talk about localization of function, while inaccurate, was crudely prophetic of things to come.

The reasons are by now probably apparent for bringing together such a weird assortment of eccentrics as Behmen, Paracelsus, Bruno, Mesmer, Spurzheim – and them only as representative of a legion of others – within the bracket of Coleridge's interest. It is not only that by temperament and out of his own miseries he tended to become counsel for the defence of originals, oddities, and outcasts. With Behmen's pantheist views as with the Paracelsian brashness and inconsistency he was in profound disagreement; by Bruno he was mystified, awesomely, by the difficulty of his writing and the immense reach of mind; by Mesmer and Spurzheim he was also mystified, for other reasons and less awesomely. One sees, however, that with or without rational agreement or emotional concern, he discussed a fellow-author or prophet with an amazing capacity for penetration to the basic issues, whatever the subject. Gold was separated from dross in each case. In addition, with less than no interest in fads and fancies, there was in Coleridge a sceptical resistance on the one hand to the prejudices of professional establishments, and on the other to the too-glib pre-judgements by the public of new concepts of men dubbed 'visionaries.' What is too little credited to Coleridge is a fine capacity for an individual provisional, tentative judgement.

53

He fully realized that the imaginative mind wherever it performs, in philosophy, or science, or religion or politics or art, will be disturbing. As the painter, Samuel Palmer, Coleridge's contemporary, knew, Imagination frightens people. But Coleridge was a chip off the old block – and if one may parody Churchill, some chip, some block. For old John Coleridge, in the 1750s before Samuel Taylor Coleridge was born, said in defending the prophet Micah against the charge of idolatry, 'Perhaps the power of vision in the prophets may be ... a new power of the mind, or a new sense awakened in them.'[10] STC's loyalty to learning and truth was absolute, but like father, like son, he yearned for and defended men with 'powers of vision.'

In the next lecture I shall attempt to say something about Coleridge's own poetic and philosophic imagination, especially as seen in the notebooks.

10 EHC in 'Biographical Notes' in *Coleridge: Studies by Several Hands* &c ed Edmund Blunden and Earl Leslie Griggs (1934) 9

※❀※ LECTURE THREE ※❀※

WILLIAM PALEY, one of those eighteenth-century divines whose cast of mind Coleridge had not much use for, had a habit he called 'skirmishing.' He had a voracious appetite, and it seems that when he had eaten everything on the table he made raids on the side dishes. This he called 'skirmishing.' Some of you I dare say have been thinking that all we have been doing is skirmishing and may be wondering about the main courses. It is I suppose the general view that those are the poems, the literary criticism, perhaps the philosophy. I shall say something about these, but I should like also to describe if I can what in that glittering eye has held me with the victimized Wedding Guest sitting on that stone beating my breast for more than forty years.

May I recapitulate briefly?

We have looked at a developing scepticism in Coleridge's childhood and youth, based on a more than usually sensitive and disillusioning conflict in him between a sense of the outward appearance of things and inner experiences – the family not familial, the church not always religious, society often anti-social in any responsible sense, and political England waving banners of self-righteous freedom against the French abroad and introducing the gagging bills and suspending the Habeas Corpus Act at home. So the development of radical critical protest – against family, university, the established church, and a repressive government was inevitable, healthy and active.

Alongside the doubts and negations there was, however, a positive reaching out towards radical thinkers of other times and countries who, out of *their* isolation and conflicts, pulled Coleridge's mind out towards wider, less insular horizons –

towards Europe – towards other disciplines, and other ways of thinking. They challenged him, as the eighteenth-century English schools and universities of his day with their limited classical emphasis and standards would never have done – to pursue the interrelatedness of all humane studies.

It was no doubt a part of their attraction for him that his favourite 'revolutionary minds' all thought and at times wrote poetically. Their language was often, to the detriment of their popularity, poetical, and some sort of imaginative resolution of external and internal was to be found in their work. So though in the last lecture we were watching intellectual processes that had scientific goals as well, we have never been far away from the poet.

The poet and the philosopher in Coleridge were one and the same man. Some professional philosophers will say that is just what was wrong with his philosophy. However that may be, it is time we stopped dividing Coleridge into departments as if he were a university. He coined the word 'interpenetration' and though he did not apply it to his own closely intercommunicating sensibilities and thoughts, we should do well so to apply it.

First of all may I categorically deny the old stuff and nonsense about the metaphysician having killed the poet in Coleridge. I thought no one now entertained that baseless, psychologically unsound piece of perversity since Sir Edmund Chambers propagated it in his hostile biography, but it turned up in a review just the other day. The poet died on 25 July 1834, with all his other departments. It is true his versifying energy diminished after 1802, roughly after the triumph of *Dejection: An Ode*, though there were some fine later spurts after that. We do not read often enough poems like *The Pang More Sharp than All*, *Time, Real & Imaginary*, *Youth & Age*, *Work without Hope*, *Love's Apparition & Evanishment*, and the interesting *Garden of Boccaccio*, though admittedly some of the

titles themselves suggest a nostalgia for something lost. But take for instance the terse lines entitled *Song* – have these not some of Meredith's sharp bitterness?

> Though veiled in spires of myrtle-wreath,
> Love is a sword which cuts its sheath,
> And through the clefts itself has made,
> We spy the flashes of the blade.
>
> But through the clefts itself has made
> We likewise see love's flashing blade,
> By rust consumed, or snapt in twain;
> And only hilt and stump remain.

That was written in 1825.

So far as the poet did wither, it was from personal misery combined with the destructive effects of opium addiction and its physical and neural accompaniments. In 1801 it is true he had said, 'The Poet is dead in me – my imagination (or rather the Somewhat that had been imaginative) lies, like a Cold Snuff on the circular Rim of a Brass Candle-stick, without even a stink of Tallow to remind you that it was once cloathed & mitred with Flame. That is past by!'[1]

But that was a letter to Godwin in which he described a three months' illness with rheumatic fever. (It is referred to in other letters also.)

I fear, your Tragedy [Godwin had sent him an unsuccessful play for criticism] will find me in a very unfit state of mind to sit in Judgement on it. I have been, during the last 3 months, undergoing a process of intellectual *exsiccation*. In my long Illness I had compelled into hours of Delight many a sleepless, painful hour of Darkness by chasing down

1 25 March 1801 to Godwin: *CL* II 713-14

metaphysical Game – and since then I have continued the Hunt, till I found myself unaware at the Root of Pure Mathematics – and up that tall smooth Tree, whose few poor Branches are all at it's very summit, am I climbing by pure adhesive strength of arms and thighs – still slipping down, still renewing my ascent. – You would not know me – ! all sounds of similitude keep at such a distance from each other in my mind, that I have *forgotten* how to make a rhyme – I look at the Mountains (that visible God Almighty that looks in at all my windows) I look at the Mountains only for the Curves of their outlines; the Stars, as I behold them, form themselves into Triangles – and my hands are scarred with scratches from a Cat, whose back I was rubbing in the Dark in order to see whether the sparks from it were refrangible by a Prism. The Poet is dead in me –

He adds that he will do what he can but –

Taste and Feeling have I none, but what I have, give I unto thee. – But I repeat, that I am unfit to decide on any but works of severe Logic.

This has been sometimes read in the old fallacious way, 'cum hoc ergo propter hoc,' but Coleridge clearly tells us himself, if we take him seriously, where the truth lies. Whereas metaphysical and logical 'game' could be pursued as an escape from physical pain and personal anxieties in those unhappy months in Greta Hall, he then could neither respond fully to natural beauty nor cope with the emotional involvement in making poems. The wear and tear of the 'visitations' of 'afflictions' had been too great. 'The Poet,' he was to say later on, after the destructive experiences of many such miseries, 'the poet calls the whole soul of man into activity.'[2]

2 *Biographia Literaria* ch XIV

The notion that philosophy killed the poet arose in part from the letter to Godwin, and in part from that lovely poem, *Dejection*. At the beginning of the poem he watches the evening sky and longs for the oncoming storm as a relief from his own 'heartless mood.' I quote some lines from the first version of the poem as sent to Sara Hutchinson. (Note that the word *genial* in Coleridge's use means having to do with his own self or nature – it does not refer to a high opinion of himself as a genius, nor to *geniality*; note also how the poem moves back and forth between outer and inner worlds.)

III

My genial spirits fail;
And what can these avail
To lift the smothering weight from off my breast?
It were a vain endeavor,
Though I should gaze for ever
On that green light that lingers in the west!
I may not hope from outward forms to win
The passion and the life, whose fountains are within!

In the next stanza a poet's need of an inner strength is under-lined. (I shall irritate those who know the poem well by selecting certain lines.)

IV

Ah! from the soul itself must issue forth
A light, a glory, a fair luminous cloud
Enveloping the Earth –
And from the soul itself must there be sent
A sweet and potent voice, of its own birth,
Of all sweet sounds the life and element!

V

O pure of heart! thou need'st not ask of me
What this strong music in the soul may be!
What, and wherein it doth exist,
This light, this glory, this fair luminous mist,
This beautiful and beauty-making power.
     Joy, virtuous Lady! Joy that ne'er was given,
Save to the pure, and in their purest hour,
Life and Life's effluence, cloud at once and shower,
Joy, Lady! is the spirit and the power,
Which wedding Nature to us gives in dower
     A new Earth and new Heaven,
Undreamt of by the sensual and the proud –
Joy is the sweet voice, Joy the luminous cloud –
     We in ourselves rejoice!
And thence flows all that charms or ear or sight,
     All melodies the echoes of that voice,
All colours a suffusion from that light.

VI

There was a time when, though my path was rough,
     This joy within me dallied with distress,
And all misfortunes were but as the stuff
     Whence Fancy made me dreams of happiness:
For hope grew round me, like the twining vine,
And fruits, and foliage, not my own, seemed mine.
But now afflictions bow me down to earth:
Nor care I that they rob me of my mirth;
          But oh! each visitation
Suspends what nature gave me at my birth,
     My shaping spirit of Imagination.
For not to think of what I needs must feel,
     But to be still and patient, all I can;

> And haply by abstruse research to steal
>> From my own nature all the natural man –
>> This was my sole resource, my only plan:
> Till that which suits a part infects the whole,
> And now is almost grown the habit of my soul.[3]

The 'abstruse research' was the mathematical and metaphysical game referred to in the letter to Godwin as a resource against sleeplessness, but 'the natural man,' as the first very personal version of the poem makes clear, was the flesh and blood man in hopeless love with Sara Hutchinson, unmistakably the old Adam.

Not only did metaphysical ideas not destroy the poet, they are actually incorporated into the poem, which is unharmed as poetry by noticing that several lines are an anticipation of a central tenet of Coleridge's thinking, the idea of what he called 'the initiative.' For a dynamic vitalism like his, the basic principle of all life was a mysterious energy behind all creation not to be sufficiently explained by any material science. The same initiative energy was the mental and emotional antecedent necessary to the creation of a poem, or any work of art:

> Ah from the soul itself must issue forth
> A light, a glory ...

and so on.

The great thing about that poem is that it was written at all. The very moment of suffering the sense of the death of poetry in himself is made into a glowing poem, in which the last stanza is a marvellous triumph of out-going selfless love over inward-looking despair:

3 George Whalley *Coleridge and Sara Hutchinson and the Asra Poems* (1955) 165-8

'Tis midnight, but small thoughts have I of sleep:
Full seldom may my friend such vigils keep!
Visit her, gentle Sleep! with wings of healing,
    And may this storm be but a mountain-birth,
May all the stars hang bright above her dwelling,
    Silent as though they watched the sleeping Earth!
        With light heart may she rise,
        Gay fancy, cheerful eyes,
    Joy lift her spirit, joy attune her voice;
To her may all things live, from pole to pole,
Their life the eddying of her living soul! ...
    O simple spirit, guided from above,
Dear Lady! friend devoutest of my choice,
Thus mayest thou ever, evermore rejoice.

Much has been written about the failure to complete *Christabel*. Wordsworth claimed that it was because Coleridge didn't know how to end it, whereas Gillman records the finished story as Coleridge told it to him; Wordsworth has had the larger audience despite Coleridge's positive statements to the contrary. The probable truth is suggested in a late notebook entry, written on his birthday in October 1823. (Not a month for swimming, except for the resolute.) He had just had a bathe in the sea at Ramsgate and 'felt the benefit ... Were I free to do so, I feel as if I could compose the third part of *Christabel*, or the song of her desolation' (Notebook 30).

But he could not write the song of her desolation, if my surmises are correct, because he was identified all too personally with that desolation. He was unable to achieve that degree of detachment he knew was necessary to the writing of poetry – and which he so eloquently admired in Shakespeare.

The proposed ending of cantos four and five was impossible to him for the opposite reason. It was to have been a sort of

All's Well That Ends Well, with the return of Christabel's lover, the defeat of the spirits of evil, and a reconciliation between father and daughter – in short a restoration generally of broken human relationships. That was an ending conceivable in his own hopes in 1798, but now twenty-five years later it was not one with which he could identify himself. So neither sufficient detachment on the one hand, nor the right kind of happy empathy on the other, was present.

The change in mood inflicted by the years is perfectly symbolized in what happened to the image of the single leaf. I suppose the most vivid symbol for Christabel herself in everyone's memory is 'the one red leaf'

> The one red leaf, the last of its clan
> That dances as often as dance it can.
> Hanging so light, and hanging so high
> On the topmost twig that looks up at the sky.

That was written in 1798. In the single dancing leaf, then, and the upward look to the sky, there was a brightness even in the rhythm in contrast to the sinister portent of the evil about to cause Christabel's desolation. A quite different single leaf, in prose a decade later, is instructive. A poor forsaken girl has endured three nights of hunger, solitude, and exposure, and finally finds temporary shelter:

As when a withered Leaf, that has been long whirled about by the gusts of Autumn, is blown into a Cave or hollow Tree, it stops suddenly, and all at once looks the very image of quiet. Such might this poor Orphan appear to the eye of a meditative imagination.[4]

When Coleridge wrote the first part of *Christabel* the

4 *Friend (CC)* II 178

outward-gazing meditative imagination was the same exuberant 'shaping spirit' which informed *The Ancient Mariner.* Ten years later the single leaf was a withered one, caught in a cave or the hollow of a tree; a casual death. Among English poets I wonder if Coleridge has an equal in the ability (even in a reduced state of creativity) to seize upon the simple, concrete, apposite image which so deeply charges thought and feeling as to become a symbol of extensive range?

This ability to see the concrete object in significant poetical terms – to absorb and be absorbed in the world of nature sufficiently to articulate it objectively and musically, made him the poet of *The Ancient Mariner.* There the perpetual systaltic movement between the Mariner's inner world of guilt, fear, remorse, penitence, disgust, utter loneliness, and the world of the elements; the sea, the storm-blast, the ice mast-high, the fog, the tyrannous sun and the awful tropical calm and drought – as I say the alternating back and forth movement between these is eloquent of that reconcilement of the internal with the external which is one of Coleridge's descriptions of art.

I suppose hardly anyone will deny that in *The Rime of the Ancient Mariner* the reconciliation of the oppositions of inner and outer worlds does marvellously take place, however much we might differ about the full meaning of the resolutions. But I find it difficult to assent to Cassirer's more general point, that 'To poeticize philosophy and to philosophize poetry ... was the highest aim of all the romantic thinkers.' What is poeticized in the *Ancient Mariner* (a rather disagreeable word, *poeticize* and unColeridgian) is experience of life, not a philosophical theory.

In a brilliant chapter (in a book with which I must disagree otherwise a good deal) Elisabeth Schneider writes illuminatingly on the music and mystery of *Kubla Khan.* She says that *Kubla Khan* presents no reconciliations but only ' "oscillation", perfectly poeticized, and possibly ironically commemorative of the author.'[5]

Now the last phrase – ' "oscillation" … possibly ironically commemorative of the author' delivers the kind of thrust at Coleridge that admirers of Hazlitt are prone to – the charge of incompleteness, indefiniteness, or oscillation, whatever one wishes to call it. And the charge be it noted is levelled usually not so much against the Coleridge who wrote poems – except for the ones he didn't write or complete – as against his mind, his work in general, his tolerance of his own inconclusiveness, his tendency to inquire and then to set aside the original question for another, and another. His lack of system admittedly is irritating to certain tempers, perhaps especially to the curriculum-making academic mind. And Coleridge is shameless about it. In a manuscript fragment he recorded:

… Southey once said to me: You are nosing every nettle along the Hedge, while the Greyhound (meaning himself, I presume) wants only to get sight of the Hare and Flash – strait as a line! he has it in his mouth! – Even so, I replied, might a Cannibal say to an Anatomist, whom he had watched dissecting a body. But the fact is – I do not care two pence for the *Hare*; but I value most highly the excellencies of scent, patience, discrimination, free Activity; and find a Hare in every Nettle I make myself acquainted with. I follow the Chamois-Hunters, and seem to set out with the same Object. But I am no Hunter of *that* Chamois Goat; but avail myself of the Chace in order to [pursue] a nobler purpose – that of making a road across the Mountain in which Common Sense may hereafter pass backward and forward, without desperate Leaps or Balloons that soar indeed but do not improve the chance of getting onward. [*IS* § 114]

The notebooks and the marginalia in particular, as we are

5 Elisabeth Schneider *Coleridge, Opium and Kubla Khan* (1953) 288

beginning to know them better, are making us increasingly acquainted with this nettle-nosing spirit in Coleridge, and more fully aware of its implications.

In the prose as in the poems – whatever the hare and however thick the nettles – what we see is a sense of the same determination to question the facts of the relatedness of inner and outer worlds. This relatedness is there, whether one sees him as being in a state of perpetual oscillation as Elisabeth Schneider does, or mumbling about *sumbject* or *ombject* as Carlyle did, or employing the polarity principle everywhere in a 'tenacious unity' as inevitable relation of creator and creature, as Owen Barfield learnedly and elegantly does, or whether one accepts Tom McFarland's analysis of a confrontation and interpenetration of the 'I AM' and the 'it is.'

It is more often than not suggested by his admirers, often the more learned and sympathetic, that Coleridge for all his brilliance lacked some sense of organization in philosophy, some architectonic power, that he built no consistent philosophical system, that he throws out wonderful aperçus but is unable or unwilling to pursue them to their logical limits, just as he was unable to complete *Christabel*. Perhaps there were some of the same causes behind both. The philosophical incompleteness and inconclusiveness on paper, however, is not a mirror-view of his mind. The notebooks alone suggest the multitudinousness of his mental and emotional life ('My thoughts crowd each other to death') – and that the pressure and strenuousness of that concentration and excitement was too much even for a man of no ordinary mental strength. And Coleridge's resilience and physical energy were remarkable. Yet partly the incompleteness of poems and philosophy may lie in the same frustration.

This is not to beg the question of whether or not Coleridge was a systematic philosopher. He referred often enough to 'my System,' most often in opposition to Schelling's, and other German transcendentalists – Fichte or Steffens – but I doubt if it can be shown from any fusion of the various fragmentary drafts that Coleridge left a systematic philosophy in the commonly accepted sense. (Possibly Thomas McFarland will do so in his edition of the unpublished *Opus Maximum*.) Even in some of his longer marches, the trail is not always pursued far enough, the logical deductions and inductions are not specific enough, to make his whole intention clear. He is not strict enough to satisfy some kinds of professional philosophers, and sometimes he is clearly grinding theological axes. Some of his attempts to draw up elaborate systematic outlines neatly divided into compartments look like attempts to challenge other writers rather than a natural initiative of his own. I have not counted the drafts of philosophical schemata, but the very number and variety may be sufficient indication of Coleridge's difficulty. Or do they indicate an unconscious disinclination to produce a single complete philosophical system?

Possibly working constantly in the notebooks gives one a more vivid impression of the struggling process than of the ultimate whole. Yet there was that description of the aim in the *Lyrical Ballads*, to depict 'the primary laws of our nature,' and, as he said in the Prospectus to the *Philosophical Lectures*, to see these laws in relation to 'the origin and primary laws of the World.' Coleridge's thought was not really fragmentary. It was organic, not a mechanical construction. That is part of the difficulty, his and ours. Perhaps his best influence lay in trying to persuade us that knowledge must be grasped with a comprehensive awareness of the interrelatedness of what he called the '*multeity*' of external and internal elements. And the impossibility of assigning him to any one school – German transcendentalist, British idealist, French existentialist or any other – is another indication of where his contribution lies. He has debts to or affinities with all of these, and with other thinkers as different as Heraclitus, Plotinus, Duns Scotus, Vico, and Schiller and Kant as well as all those post-Kantian transcendentalists he read so assiduously. (My count is about fifty volumes of them – he probably read them more widely than anyone of his time in England.) He read them critically, chiefly to make use of their vast compendia of natural and philosophical history, but he was the incorrigible questioner of their fixed positions, discriminatingly syncretic, rather than eclectic.

Sir Isaiah Berlin has said: 'The importance of philosophers in the end resides in the fact that the issues which they raised are live issues still (or again), and ... have not perished with the vanished societies in which they were conceived.'[6] He was writing about Vico, whom Coleridge greeted when he was given a copy of the *New Science* in 1825 (he read it in the Italian) as a kindred spirit, because Vico also had been trying to understand the primary laws of human nature, looking at myths and symbols of earlier ages as the products of social changes and revaluations. Coleridge too was looking for a philosophy of man. His difficulty was that he could leave nothing out of his inquiries. The validity of many of those inquiries persists today, however, for if they have one central fire it is the conviction that philosophy and religion arise out of human need, that that need is not entirely rational nor to be satisfied completely by reason, and that therefore exploration of the complexities of the inner world of the human consciousness, of the social world of man, and of the physical world of science, must all eventually be viewed together. Investigation for him must originate with the inward,[7] and then move outwards.

In 1809 he wrote in Notebook 25:

6 *Vico and Herder* (1975) xvi
7 As in his plan for Wordsworth's Philosophical Poem: *Table Talk* 21 July 1832

If it were asked of me to justify the interest ... the majority of the best and noblest minds feel in the great questions – Where am I? What and for what am I? What are the duties, which arise out of the relations of my Being to itself as heir of futurity, and to the World which is its present sphere of action and impression? – I would compare the human Soul to a Ship's Crew cast on an unknown Island (a fair Simile: for these questions could not suggest themselves unless the mind had previously felt convictions, that the present World was not its whole destiny and abiding Country) – what would be their first business? Surely, to enquire <what the Island was? in what Latitude?> what ships visited that Island? when? and whither they went? – and what chance that they should take off first one, & then another? – and after this – to think, how they should maintain & employ themselves during their stay – & how best stock themselves for the expected voyage, & procure the means of inducing the Captain to take them to the Harbour, which they wished to go to? –

The moment, when the Soul begins to be sufficiently self-conscious, to ask concerning itself, & its relations, is the first moment of its *intellectual* arrival into the World – Its *Being* – enigmatic as it must seem – is posterior to its *Existence*. – Suppose the ship-wrecked man stunned, & for many weeks in a state of Ideotcy or utter loss of Thought & Memory – & then gradually awakened. [*CN* III 3593]

'Hope and Fear suppose an unknown yet real certainty' he said – 'the fixed and necessary Relation of Object to Subject' (*CN* III 3592). But what that 'Relation' was remained his question. All knowing was for him a creative ordering of chaos, and therefore, he said, 'the Necessary and Immutable is the central point to which all human knowlege gravitates' (ibid). Yet as 'a repetition in the finite mind of the Infinite I AM,' whatever is humanly created is a struggling repetition, at a distance, enduring the limitations and the comparative relativity that are the conditions of human frailty. So although as a Cambridge philosopher, Dorothy Emmet, says, '... few professional philosophers have seen as far as Coleridge into the powers of the human mind,'[8] or perhaps because of that, Coleridge on his own hypothesis would have found it difficult to be the architect of a complete system.

... He believed in growth, the 'free life', with a deep antipathy to 'the confining form'; he had what he called a 'rooted aversion to the *Arbitrary*'; systems and system-making do tend to become at some point arbitrary. He preferred 'method' to system, and it will be protested by some that he did not achieve method either. But that depends on what you mean by it. He said somewhere that the shortest path gives one the knowledge best, but the longer way round makes one more knowing. The fragments he left us in such quantities certainly necessitate the longer way round. They tantalize us into wishing to understand him, and then, willy-nilly, into facing the questions he raised.[9]

I have been quoting myself. And now I should like to share more directly, albeit in their own miscellaneousness, the chaos of the notebooks.

On the subject of his insistence on, even obsession with the necessity of establishing the relations of things, and the difficulties created thereby, he made this private admission:

Doubtless it would visit the Realm of Literature with a plusquam polar Ink-frost, if a man were bound to write on nothing till he understood everything! Nevertheless, so far I hold it a possible and expedient approximation that, no other person having done it for me, I strive to begin at the Beginning. But independent of the probable unsatisfactory nature of the results, I am yearly more and

8 'Coleridge and Philosophy' in *S. T. Coleridge* ed R.L. Brett (Writers and Their Background Series 1971) 196

9 *The Self-Conscious Imagination* (1974) 76-7

more sensible of the *difficulty* of writing on detached Subjects (Philo-
sophical subjects I mean, whether physio- theo- or anthropo-logical)
and whenever from whatever motive I make the attempt, the impor-
tance of this, that, and yet another and another Principle, or Posi-
tion, which had I proceeded to the Subject as part of the *System*, I
should have enunciated a half or a whole Volume before, and from
frequent previous applications of the Principle have needed only a
few words and a (Vide § – p. –) the sense, I say, of the necessity of
some higher *formula* is sure to return and harrass me with its Solicit-
ings, like a night-traveller who every two or three minutes makes a
stop and then walks on with his head over his shoulder, because he
hears, or fancies that he hears someone behind, panting and calling
out his name, some auditual Jack a' Lanthorn, or *Vox Fatua*. [*IS* §
167]

I would point out that most of all that is one sentence, so the
difficulty is not only detaching subjects but detaching sen-
tences. He often made fun of himself for his weakness for
parentheses.

One aspect of these closely knit passages is the swiftness of
his own association of ideas, which sometimes brings together
marvellous incongruities. For instance, in Notebook 22 we
find this:

31 March 1817. Highgate. – Monday Morning, six o'clock. *Hen Pen*
[Henry Gillman, 2 or 3 years old] resenting the being washed, in the
nursery, opposite the drawing Room in which I sit.

I will not say, that in our present religious controversies we are
disputing about *trifles*… [*CN* III 4341]

One might think that the association (if any) was in the word
trifles, which is italicized, little Henry Gillman's objections to
the trifling business of being washed. But the entry goes on
about Original Sin and man's alienation from God –

We must be away from Him / for an omnipotent Father would never suffer an *innocent* Son to be tormented in his presence ...

Now Coleridge had a fatherly affection for Henry Gillman and a special understanding of him, a problem child, and I suggest (it is perhaps blasphemous) – that Coleridge could not bear hearing his screams over having a dirty face washed, and that this somehow linked up easily with God's suffering over the original filth of man. Everything *is* related to everything else. The entry continues with the Prodigal Son, Heaven not a place, Unitarianism and Materialism.

Coleridge had a taste for the incongruous analogy, especially against pompous politicians; particularly he despised much of what passed in parliament for logic. (Historians would do well to look in on Coleridge occasionally; they might find some amusing memoranda on public affairs.)

Thursday 15 May 1823 – Debate in the House of Commons on Mr. Fowell Buxton's Motion for the Emancipation of Negro Slaves, whose speech, a something between a College Declamation, and the opening Harangue of the Counsel for a Prosecution at the old Bailey, ... was answered by Mr. Canning with his wonted ability and adroitness, and likewise with his wonted Sophistry and dexterous Quid-pro-quo-ism. [Notebook 29]

Coleridge copied out a long piece of the debate:

... Mr. C. confessed that he always had a decided objection to the introduction of the Name of Christianity in the debates of the House. *(In this I perfectly agree with Mr. C.)*

After more about Christianity and the slave trade Canning said:

74

It is true there is no permission in the Chr. Doctrine for the infliction of Slavery, but it was not true that there was any direct *prohibition* of it.

Coleridge inserted a parenthesis in his notes, suddenly remembering similar logic in a schoolfellow who defended a friend caught smoking a cigar:

(*Mem. Winch's Defence of* [*Blank*] *and leaving the Sin offering in full fume on Bowyer's Desk.* 'You know, Sir! You never forewarned it'. S.T.C.)

The bad logic of the public men of his time was frequently the subject of Coleridge's anger and laughter.

A quite different tone running through all the notebooks may surprise those who know only the more formal works: namely that tentativeness I have already mentioned. The very titles he gave some of his notebooks suggest the mood: 'Fly-catcher or Day-Book for impounding stray thoughts' (Notebook 45) or '*Volatilia*, or Day-book for bird-liming small Thoughts – impounding Stray Thoughts and holding for Trial doubtful Thoughts.' In a late entry, for example, Coleridge said (1829):

Should these pages in their present state in consequence of death or disablement preventing me from arriving at a fuller & clear insight, meet the eye of an intelligent Reader, let him know that he cannot be more sensible than I myself am, of the turbidness and obscurity of the preceding imperfect exposition of the thought ... etc. etc. [Notebook 39]

The serious side of this can be very disarming. He is willing to change his mind even about things of major importance to him. Parliamentary Reform, for instance.

You cannot conceive how this Corn Bill haunts me – and so it would you if you had seen the pale faces and heard the conversation of the hundred poor Creatures [he was writing in 1815 from Somerset] who came to sign the Petition. Except Horner every one of the opponents of the measure has betrayed the Cause ... The North is in a flame – the result will be a league between the Ministry and the Land-Nabobs not to disband the Soldiery. [He clearly, like some others, feared civil war.] I have hitherto in the Friend in the M. Post and the Courier, and in conversation, opposed the so called Parliament Reformers – I have not altered my *principles* – yet now I must join in pleading for Reform. – I assumed as the Ideal of a Legislature – that in which all the great component interests of the State are adequately represented, so that no one should have the power of oppressing the others, the whole being in sympathy of action & re-action with the feelings and convictions of the People – I now see that this is not the case – & I see the historical cause too. – Neither Blackstone or De Lolme have truly given the Theory of our Constitution – which would have been realized in practice but for two oversights. – But of this hereafter –. I have no opportunity of seeing any of the Shoal of Pamphlets on this Question; but I suppose, that the Speeches in Parliament contain the Essence – if so, God have mercy on the Intellects of the Nation! How indeed can it be otherwise, with such Educations as our Gentlemen receive! [*CL* IV 553-4]

There is a certain reasonableness about Coleridge, an ability to reconsider; he is the true inquirer. Born into the Church of England, in the 1790s a Unitarian, and for the rest of his life highly critical of the Church of England as an institution, Coleridge nevertheless returned to it again, and for the first time since his Cambridge days, took the Sacrament in 1827. Yet the question of necessitarianism gave him trouble. Having renounced it himself he still, in 1810, wrote in a notebook:

I dare avow – & hope, I shall give no offence to serious Believers – that it appears to me scarcely possible, that a young man of ingenuous dispositions, warm sensibility, and an enquiring mind should avoid Socinianism. [*CN* III 3743]

By which he means necessitarian Unitarianism. He works out at some length five reasons, the most interesting of which was that the young feel no need of the doctrine of free will –

we least value & think of that which we enjoy in the highest degree – this free-agency, the unsettled state of Habit not yet Tyranny – we begin to think of & intellectually know, our freedom, when we have been made to feel its imperfections and its loss. [*CN* III 3743]

In another entry a little later he specifically relates this last point to himself as a young man.

What was my own case has so often come within my observation in others that I am almost disposed to generalize it into a rule – that the more vigorous the Volition, (as in sanguine lively young men of quick abilities) the less the indisposition to the denial of the Free will and the doctrine of Necessity or absolute preformation of every possible act in the one causa causarum – Nay, that from the same law of mind at the aera in which we are most rich in any thing, that thing we least *stickle* for. The young *think* more highly of chastity than the Man of 50-60. – [Notebook 27]

In 1795 in a Bristol lecture, reprinted in *The Friend*, he had cogently advocated necessitarianism; then, over twenty years later, in at least three copies of *The Friend* he wrote a marginal note:

I hope, that this paragraph in all the fullness of its Contrast with my present Convictions, will start up before me whenever I speak, think, or feel *intolerantly* of Persons on account of their doctrines and opinions.' 'S.T. Coleridge. Highgate, 30 Octr 1818' [*Friend (CC)* I 338]

There was a related entry six years later.

In 1824, his son Derwent showed signs of free-thinking, apparently, but it was combined with a certain flashiness and worldliness that bothered his father.

Mem. of the aera of Phil. Necess. with me my true Lehrjahre. The World, man included, not the object; but God i.e. Good, Truth, Beauty + a Power limited only by its identity with G.T. and B. – Such was the beautiful half-truth that deceived & saved me. But D. & his Perverters! –O! – [Notebook 29]

Derwent eventually became ultra-respectable and High Church in spite of the fact that one of his 'Perverters' was Thomas Babington Macaulay.

Part of the pleasure of the notebooks is such glimpses of Coleridge's candour, changing his mind about *Necessity* and trying to understand and to explain himself to himself and the young men around him to themselves: even the sign, in the 1824 entry about Derwent, of the old man's affection for his own past, though self-indulgent, has something human about it. Besides, the contrast with Derwent was a true one: Coleridge's radical youth was never self-seeking, never anything but idealistic, and there was concern in more than one quarter about Derwent's lack of seriousness in his twenties.

Something one never tires of is the unexpected observations, often in no particular context, just the original thoughts of an observant man. Examples are legion, of which I take but a small sample:

When balloons, or these new roads, upon which they say it will be possible to travel fifteen miles an hour, for a day together, shall become the common mode of travelling, women will become more locomotive; – the health of all classes will be materially benefitted. Women will then spend less time in attiring themselves – will invent some more simple head gear, or dispense with it altogether.[10]

Or again,

I feel that there is a mystery in the sudden by-act-of-will-unaided, nay, more than that, frustrated, recollection of a Name. I was trying to recollect the name of a Bristol Friend, who had attended me in my Illness at Mr Wade's. I began with the Letters of the Alphabet – A B C & c. – and I know not why, felt convinced that it began with H. I ran thro' all the vowels, aeiouy, and with all the consonants to each – Hab, Heb, Hib, Hob, Hub and so on – in vain. I then began other Letters – all in vain. Three minutes afterwards, having completely given it up, the name, Daniel, at once started up, perfectly insulated, without any the dimmest antecedent connection, as far as my consciousness extended. There is no explanation, ὡς ἐμοίγε δοκεῖ, of this fact, but by a full sharp distinction of Mind from Consciousness – the Consciousness being the narrow *Neck* of the Bottle. The name, Daniel, must have been a living *Atom*-thought in my mind, whose uneasy motions were the craving to recollect it – but the very craving led the mind to a search which at each successive disappointment (= a tiny pain) tended to contract the orifice or *outlet* into Consciousness. Well – it is given up – & all is quiet – the Nerves are asleep, or off their guard – & then the Name pops up, makes its way, & there it is! – not assisted by any association, but the very contrary – by the suspension and *sedation* of all associations. [*IS* § 3]

What some persons enjoy most in Coleridge's prose, in the notebooks and letters particularly, also in the marginalia, are his pithy aphorisms, often in inquiry form. For example,

10 Thomas Allsop *Letters, Conversations and Recollections of S. T. Coleridge* (1836) II 154

Is it or is it not true, that whoever supermoralizes unmoralizes? [*CN* II 2358]

[Agreeing with Leibniz that] Men's errors (intellectual) consist chiefly in *denying*. [*CN* II 2596]

[A favourite image] – It is not enough that we have once swallowed it – the *Heart* should have *fed* upon the *truth*, as insects on a Leaf, till it be tinged with the colour, and shew its food in every minutest fibre. [*CL* I 115]

[On the rejection of new ideas] – Incredulity is but credulity seen from behind, bowing and nodding assent to the Habitual & Fashionable. [*SM* (*CC*) Appendix C 81]

Minds that feel and struggle up against the weight and witchery of Custom. [Notebook 29]

A Tyrant is only a Monstrous Phantasm up-steaming from the Grave and Corruption of the huddled Corses of the self-murdered Virtue & inner freedom of the People – i.e. the Majority of the Citizens of the State. [Notebook 29]

The defect of Archbishop Leighton's reasoning is taking Eternity for a kind of time. [Notebook 21½]

We can scarcely think too highly of the potential in us, or too humbly of the Actual. [Marginal note on Schlegel, *Athenaeum* I i.77]

Naturally some of the most interesting entries are about himself. He had been writing about the need for humility, but, he says

preserve me from the deadly Hensbane of Self-contempt, the worst <and> most concentrated form of Selfishness! For it is a shrinking down into the mere Self, an abstraction from the redeeming God. It is well to know & feel what we *should* be without God. But to contemplate our Self as actually existing without God, is frightful morally, & a contradiction philosophically ... [Notebook 44]

or again –

what Method should a Philosopher and Thinker adopt to form or to cultivate – Habits of Religious Feeling? [Notebook 26]

About the opium-taking he expresses himself rather conventionally perhaps, but he sees that although opium was one of the stumbling blocks to self-knowledge, and creative activity generally, yet he asks himself, has it been also one of the pressures towards self-examination, a door towards secret passages – to curious states of insight into other human beings?

Need we wonder at Plato's opinions concerning the Body, at least, need that man wonder whom a *pernicious Drug* shall make capable of conceiving & bringing forth Thoughts, hidden in him before, which shall call for the deepest feelings of his best, greatest, & sanest Contemporaries? and this proved to him by actual experience? But can subtle strings set in greater tension do this? Or is it not that the dire poison for a delusive time has made the body, i.e. the organization ... the unknown somewhat, a fitter Instrument for the all-powerful Soul? [*CN* III 3320]

The amount of sheer pain in the notebooks has been startling to many readers. (It shook for some days the late Helen Darbishire when she read the galley-proofs of volume II.) There, for instance, a long entry about his hopeless love for Sara Hutchinson ends,

Awakened from a dream of Tears, & anguish of involuntary Jealousy, ½ past 2 / Sept. 13. 1807, and it is followed by this:

To lie in ease yet dull anxiety for hours, afraid to think a thought, lest some thought of Anguish should shoot a pain athwart my body, afraid even to turn my body, lest the very bodily motion should introduce a train of painful Thoughts– [*CN* II 3149]

Two years earlier in Malta he had written:

... Who that thus lives with a continually divided Being can remain healthy! <And who can long remain body-crazed, & not at times use unworthy means of making his Body the fit instrument of his mind? Pain is easily subdued compared with continual uncomfortableness – and the sense of stifled Power! – O this is that which made poor Henderson, Collins, Boyce, &c &c &c–*Sots*! – awful Thoughts–O it is horrid! – Die, my Soul, die! – Suicide–rather than this, the worst State of Degradation! It is less a suicide! S.T.C.>–I work hard, I do the duties of common Life from morn to night / but verily–I raise my limbs, 'like lifeless *Tools*'–The organs of motion & outward action perform their functions at the stimulus of a galvanic fluid applied by the *Will*, not by the Spirit of Life that makes Soul and Body one. [*CN* II 2557]

But as I said earlier, the resilience and the sanity, so much called for, were remarkable. He says that his infirmities have been useful to him, perhaps more useful than Wordsworth's '*Anti*firmities,' in making him aware of the feelings of others, but his own words so shocked him that he entitled the entry 'A Gnostic Whisper' and wrote the most frightening words in Greek characters. I have translated and/or transliterated them in square brackets:

<*A Gnostic Whisper* Εεπτεντριονισμος [Northernism] the *genus* of which Εκοτισμος [Scotism] is the superlative *Species*, κυμβερ-

λανδισμος [Cumberlandism] a *vaccine* - Ιορκισμος [Yorkism] the middle link.>

N.B. That as far as *Philosophy* (= the Sum Total, of the Being) is concerned, *In*firmities sunk under, the Conscious Soul mourning and disapproving, are less hindrances than *Anti*firmities – such as *Self*-ness ... and *separative* instead of being, what it ought to be, at once *distinctive* and yet, at the same moment or rather act, *conjunctive*, <nay,> *unificent*! I will not refer to Αυστραλις [Australis – Southey]; but to a *truly* great GENIUS, Ἀξιόλογος [Axiologos – Wordsworth] – Were *intellect* only in question, στς [STS for STC] would rather groan under his manifold sins & sorrows, all either contained in or symbolized by, ΩΠΙΜ [OPIUM] than cherish that self-concentration <of Αξ.> [of Ax.] which renders the dearest beings *means* to him, never really *ends*. N.B. Its curious & often ludicrous effects on the *memory*. Αξ [Ax.] has more than once or twice gravely preached to στς [STC], as a new discovery, what στς [STC] had been years before attempting but in vain to persuade Αξ [Ax.] of, not only in conversation but by long Letters – but who can rearticulate the pulses of the Air? And as to the Letters, they not being those of Αξ, ηαδελφη αδελφολατρα [Ax. the brother-worshipping sister] had made thread-papers of them! – From the same source Ουιλσυν [Wilson] & the other silly Αξιολατροι [Wordsworth-idolaters] (as opposed to the true Αξιολογοσεβασται [Wordsworth-honourers]) – and from the same the *strange* feeling, (*strange* to whom the force of self-vorticity is not, or imperfectly, known) his belief, that every thought or even image coincident with one of his own *must* have been borrowed from him <in short,> = Debts forgotten, & the <very> Air of intellects respired by another a Debt to *him*! – In so truly great a mind, spite of connate σεπτεντριονίσμου; και ἀττορνιυιέτητος [northernism and attorney sonship] this could not have been A = A, had it not been fostered in reclusion in the lap of blind, shall I not say hatched by the lightless *Stove* of, *She=pansympathy* ...

[There is more of this, but the entry ends with the declaration that] AXIOLOGUS = **AΩ** [the Alpha Omega] of the living Great Men. – such is στς's [STC's] faith. [*CN* III 4243]

There is a good deal of self-inspection in the notebooks, but little of Wordsworth's 'self-concentration' or 'self-vorticity' of which Coleridge complains here.

Coleridge is objective enough to indulge in a good deal of self-persiflage –

N.B. Half a page wasted in Nonsense, and a whole page in the confutation of it. But such is the nature of exercise – I walk a mile for health – & then another to return home again. [*CN* II 2406]

Or again, he refers to

The hypochondriac, or the intemperate man, – and his endless fruitless Memoranda / fruitless and perhaps pernicious as familiarizing his mind to the Contemplation, the lazy Contemplation of his own Weakness. [*CN* II 2474]

Coleridge's concern with himself was regularly related to much larger human issues. And I suppose this is the aspect of the notebooks that makes it possible never to be bored with them.

He said his mind was early 'habituated to the Vast,' the worlds upon worlds without. We see that he was also early habituated to the Vast within, the layers upon layers of contradictory feelings, thoughts and half-thoughts, illusion and disillusion, insights and obscurities and mysteries. But the outer and inner infinites were neither divorced from nor tyrannized over by the outer and inner finites. It is the constant response and re-adjustment to these, the truly systolic-diastolic movement of heart and mind that constitutes the endless fascination of Coleridge. A certain amount of amusement has often tended to mock his preoccupation with the reconciliation of 'the One and the Many.' But as Owen Barfield succinctly put it, and the notebooks bear him out,

The problem of the one & the many was not, for him, a mere philosophical conundrum; it was the practical & moral problem of how to be a human being.[11]

11 *What Coleridge Thought* (1971) 148

Asterisks indicate quotation

89